THE LETTER TO THE ROMANS

BOOKS BY EMIL BRUNNER
Published by The Westminster Press

The Letter to the Romans
Faith, Hope, and Love
The Great Invitation, and Other Sermons
Eternal Hope
The Misunderstanding of the Church
The Christian Doctrine of Creation
    and Redemption, *Dogmatics, Vol. II*
The Scandal of Christianity
The Christian Doctrine of God,
    Dogmatics, Vol. I
Man in Revolt
The Mediator
The Divine Imperative
Revelation and Reason

The LETTER
to the
ROMANS

A Commentary

by

EMIL BRUNNER

Philadelphia

THE WESTMINSTER PRESS

English Translation © *MCMLIX Lutterworth Press*

Der Römerbrief was first published in 1938, by
J. G. Oncken Verlag of Kassel. This English translation is based upon one made by H. A. Kennedy
from the 1956 German edition. The English text
used for The Letter to the Romans is the Revised
Standard Version of the Bible, copyright, 1946
and 1952, by the Division of Christian Education
of the National Council of Churches and used
by permission.

LIBRARY OF CONGRESS CATALOG CARD No. 59-9193

TYPESET IN GREAT BRITAIN
PRINTED IN THE UNITED STATES OF AMERICA

Contents

8.5

Introduction

"THIS letter is the principal part of the New Testament and the purest gospel, which surely deserves the honour that a Christian man should not merely know it off by heart word for word, but that he should be occupied with it daily as the daily bread of the soul. For it can never be read too often and too well. And the more it is used the more delicious it becomes and the better it tastes. . . ."

With these words Martin Luther in the year 1522 began his introduction to the Letter to the Romans in the first edition of the New Testament newly translated by him. We shall hardly be tempted to take the risk of imitating him in this by saying that the Letter to the Romans is plainly the principal part of the New Testament; if one part would have to be called the principal part, then the Gospels, surely, would merit it. But we must agree with Luther in this: that the Letter to the Romans is fateful in the story of the Christian Church. Throughout the centuries of Christian history, the fate of the Church of Christ has time and again depended on the understanding and evaluation of the Letter to the Romans. Why is this? Because in this single literary document what is particular and decisive in the Christian Faith is worked out in the acutest form and presented in a concentrated, instructive manner. Within the entire New Testament, even within the whole Bible, nothing approximates so closely to a theological treatise as this epistle—although it was written as a genuine letter addressed to a definite congregation.

We know little more about this earliest period of the congregation in Rome to which Paul was writing than what we are able to deduce from this letter. The Community was founded neither by Paul nor even by one of his special fellow-workers (Timothy, Silas, etc.); in all probability not by an apostle at all. It had already existed for some time and presumably had its origin in the assembling in Rome, the

9

metropolis, of Christians from various parts of the world. It consisted of former Jews and Gentiles. On account of its life of faith it had a good name everywhere, though without taking, at that time, any leading part.

How is it that Paul is writing a letter to them?

The apostle to the Gentiles feels that his task in the East has in the main been fulfilled. The call of his Lord directs him to the West. He wants to travel to Spain via Rome, and the purpose of the letter is to serve as a preparation for his first visit to Rome. The Roman Community is to aid him in his mission to Spain; therefore he must gain its confidence and make clear to it what is in his mind concerning the proclamation of the Gospel. This accounts for the didactic character of the letter. It is not polemical like Galatians, Colossians or the second letter to the Corinthians; unlike both the letters to the Thessalonians or the first epistle to the Corinthians, it is not written mainly from a pastoral interest, or as a letter of encouragement like the one to the Philippians, but—and this is what is special about it—as a real letter of instruction. In this letter too, as in all others of Paul, there is a passionate wrestling; not with an opponent, however, or a danger within the community to which it is addressed, but with foes and perils that are found in every man and also with adversaries quite outside the Christian Community. Thus among all the epistles of Paul this is the least dated, the letter which concerns us most directly in exactly the same way as it concerned those in Rome.

The place and time of its composition we can, of course, quite definitely determine within the history of the apostle Paul, though only approximately in regard to the year. Paul is facing his last journey to Jerusalem, whither he wants to take the proceeds of the collection which he has gathered in Greece for the poor of the original Community. His third missionary journey lies behind him; his labours in the East have been concluded. In spite of this fairly accurate dating, the statements of scholars concerning the precise date fluctuate between 54 and 58 A.D. The place of composition is very probably Corinth. For a long time it was looked upon as settled among scholars that chapter 16 did not belong to the original letter, since Paul could not possibly

have had so many acquaintances in a Community unknown to him; this ending of the letter must, although un-
doubtedly deriving from Paul, have slipped by a mistake
into the epistle. To-day another opinion is held, which
regards the reasons for its belonging here as stronger than
those against. The final verses of chapter 16, on the other
hand, have in all probability been added by a later hand,
though in content they fit very well into the whole.

The structure of the letter is clear and simple. Following
the preamble, in which the apostle introduces himself and
seeks to get into touch with this Community, he at once
proceeds to the first main theme: the lost state of mankind
without the redemption of Christ, both of the Gentiles and
the Jews; they are sinners both of them. Then follows the
second main theme: the unfolding of the message of Jesus
Christ's redemption. This twofold first main part is then
followed by two more: Part Two which deals with God's
plan for the world as revealed in Christ in the light of the
Jewish people, and Part Three, which draws the consequences
from Christ's message for the practical life. At the end he
comes back again to the beginning: the apostle tells the
Roman Community about his missionary plans and assures
himself of their friendship.

That is the framework of the letter. But what life it
breathes! What a power of the Spirit must have been alive
in this Paul to have been able to dictate such a work in a
few nights. Paul has supplied the material and pointed the
way for the whole of Christian theology and all Christian
thought with these sixteen chapters. Here is said the fundamental thing about man's misery and God's help, man's
vain striving for the goal and God's wisdom and mercy,
about God's gift to all those who will receive it, and the task
arising out of this gift; and it is said in a way that no one
else could say it before Paul or since. There is probably no
document of human spiritual history where passion of feeling,
power of thought and inexorableness of will are so per-
meated by one another as here. In the face of this volcanic
original production in which everything surges red hot out
of the depths of the divine mystery of love, the cheap contrast between life and doctrine, theology and piety, passes

away. To be sure, Paul is a theological teacher and thinker; but he is one whom we cannot follow without having our whole life set in motion. To be sure, Paul is an apostle, evangelist, missionary and pastor to thousands; yet he takes time off for a few nights to summarize the Christian doctrine for a Community which he wishes to use as a base for a most audacious missionary enterprise; and all theological teaching since can draw the best from this nocturnal dictation as out of an inexhaustible reservoir.

Yet in all this the main thing has not been mentioned. In this letter of Paul to the Romans God Himself wants to speak to us. The Pauline teaching is the means through which God Himself wants to teach us; Paul's epistle to the Romans is a letter from God to us, mankind to-day. It remains the great problem of interpretation, hitherto never entirely solved, how to unite these two things: the keen attention to what Paul wanted to say to that Community then, and the search for what God wants to say to us through Paul to-day. In the end the question is whether the reader will really allow God to speak to him, or whether he evades God by hiding behind "Paul", behind "the past". The little theological dictionary at the end of the book has been written to aid the reader in this task of making it contemporary, and he may consult it profitably while still reading the exposition of the text.

Translation and Exposition
of
The Letter to the Romans

Part One

THE RIGHTEOUSNESS OF GOD THROUGH FAITH IN JESUS CHRIST (chapters 1–8)

THE APOSTLE AND HIS COMMISSION (I: 1-7)

¹Paul, a servant of Jesus Christ, called to be an apostle, set apart for the gospel of God ²which he promised beforehand through his prophets in the holy scriptures, ³the gospel concerning his Son, who was descended from David according to the flesh ⁴and designated Son of God in power according to the Spirit of holiness by his resurrection from the dead, Jesus Christ our Lord, ⁵through whom we have received grace and apostleship to bring about obedience to the faith for the sake of his name among all the nations, ⁶including yourselves who are called to belong to Jesus Christ;

⁷To all God's beloved in Rome, who are called to be saints: Grace to you and peace from God our Father and the Lord Jesus Christ.

In ancient times a letter began with the sender's name and greetings. This does the same. But one thing becomes clear at once: this man does not write in a private capacity but as the representative of his Lord. His name disappears beneath that of his principal, and his greeting contains already the great message which he has to deliver. He introduces himself as someone who has and wants nothing for himself. The commission which he has received is his life. He is a messenger and nothing else.

His mission has its basis in the ancient revelation contained in the Scriptures of the Old Testament but whose real content is actually the Son of God, the man Jesus from the tribe of David who, nevertheless, is the Son of God through the Holy Spirit, one with him in essence (Phil. 2: 6). Only through and since the resurrection from the dead, which set him free from the weakness of the flesh, has this sonship manifested itself in power. The Son is the sum and substance of the good News, for the delivery of which he, this Lord, has graciously prepared

13

and set apart Paul as his servant. It is good news for all. Although it deals with Israel's Messiah promised in the Old Testament, it is also meant for the Gentile nations; for he wants to be known and acknowledged by all as the Lord. Paul introduces himself to the Roman Community as the one who has been commissioned to win all Gentiles for Jesus. They, the Romans and he, although they have never seen one another, are from the very beginning surrounded by the one grace and love of God the Father, revealed in Christ the Lord and communicated through the Holy Spirit.

In this the theme of the whole letter is already indicated. From God's side the lordship of Christ, the revealer of God's love; from man's side the "obedience of faith". Faith is Christ really becoming my Lord, and Christ cannot become my Lord in any other way save by my knowing and my acknowledging him in whom God claims me as his own. This act of becoming Lord is God's programme for humanity and the world, which is not only to be proclaimed by his envoy but also realized by him.

THE PERSONS AND THE SUBJECT-MATTER (I: 8-17)

[8]First, I thank my God through Jesus Christ for all of you, because your faith is proclaimed in all the world. [9]For God is my witness, whom I serve with my spirit in the gospel of his Son, that without ceasing I mention you always in my prayers, [10]asking that somehow by God's will I may now at last succeed in coming to you. [11]For I long to see you, that I may impart to you some spiritual gift to strengthen you, [12]that is, that we may be mutually encouraged by each other's faith, both yours and mine. [13]I want you to know, brethren, that I have often intended to come to you (but thus far have been prevented), in order that I may reap some harvest among you as well as among the rest of the Gentiles. [14]I am under obligation both to Greeks and to barbarians, both to the wise and to the foolish: [15]so I am eager to preach the gospel to you also who are in Rome.

[16]For I am not ashamed of the gospel: it is the power of God for salvation to every one who has faith, to the Jew first and also to the Greek. [17]For in it the righteousness of God is revealed through faith for faith; as it is written, "He who through faith is righteous shall live."

The strictest objective approach is here also completely personal. First of all the apostle is grateful to God for what has happened to the Roman Community. Paul knows nothing of a faith which is so concealed that nothing of it is visible. The whole world speaks of the faith of the Roman brethren, and this calls for gratitude. The Holy Spirit who arms him for prayer and service is the same one who binds him in heart with the Christians in Rome, and so he is longing for personal fellowship with them. Fellowship, however, is mutual exchange. He too, the apostle, wants not only to give but also to receive. The apostle is no prince of the Church who only gives out, but a brother desirous of encouragement from his fellow-brethren. Yet this humble man thinks in continents as he reflects on his task. At the beginning and end of his letter he allows us to have a look at his world-embracing strategy of mission. He is the fisher of men in the grand style. Thus runs his commission from the very start (cp. Acts. 9: 15-16). How could he who, as the first to be entrusted with the mystery that the Gentiles as well as the Jews were destined for the redemption of the Messiah (Eph. 3), pass by Rome, the metropolis of the world!

What Rome meant then is almost beyond our comprehension. We must imagine as one all the capital cities of our own day together, from New York and London to Tokyo. He, the Jewish itinerant preacher, is to conquer Rome for Christ. By what means? By the message of a Galilean who was executed as a criminal! In face of the wisdom and might of Rome, to set up the "foolishness of the Cross", this glorification of the powerless one! But the apostle's thought barely touches upon what might have been so natural, namely, the failing of his courage when confronted by this contrast. There are no inferiority complexes here and no false humility, but an unbroken consciousness of power. "I am not ashamed; for it is the power of God." The Gospel is not only an epoch-making power but a power for salvation; its effect reaches into eternity, just as itself derives from eternity. Thus it is for everyone. God's truth, God's will and God's love know no frontiers; even the greatest oppositions of blood and history which split humanity apart lose all meaning in face of it. There exists only one frontier, only one exclusive condition: faith. "To everyone who has faith." Christ uses force with no one. This Lord can only

become Lord in the free obedience of faith; if there is one
thing that cannot be enforced, it is trust.

"The righteousness of God." Out of the understanding
of this phrase, whose meaning had lain buried for several
hundred years under an alien human tradition of religion, was
born the Reformation. From the moment Luther understood
again the meaning of the righteousness of God, he was called
to be the Reformer of Christendom. "Then I suddenly felt that
I was born again and entered through open doors into para-
dise", he wrote. The righteousness of God is not his judicial
righteousness but that which he royally bestows; not—as the
contrast is presented later—a righteousness from the works of
the law, but righteousness by faith. To believe means to receive.
Here it concerns the righteousness received and freely granted,
the unique righteousness founded on the gift of God. Yet in
the same way this faith is also the goal; the divine revelation
also leads to faith.

Once more the theme of the letter is indicated in a new form.
This concerns God and his will. Wherever his will is realized,
there is the righteousness of God. It is nothing else but what in
the Gospels is called the "reign of God" or the "Kingdom of
God". But this reign of God is not realized in man's own
activity but solely in the action of God. And yet it concerns
the realization of God's will among mankind, in men's lives,
and thus the action of God whereby man is delivered into the
power of God, in which the inmost resistance of man is broken
and the decisive obstacle to the dominion of God is therefore
removed.

The righteousness of God is realized in faith. He who believes
lives by God's word and action alone; he receives his life from
God's hand as a lease and he lives it as his liegeman.

A. ALL MANKIND'S NEED OF REDEMPTION
(1: 18—3: 20)

GOD'S WRATH AND JUDGMENT
ON THE GENTILES (1: 18-32)

18For the wrath of God is revealed from heaven against all
ungodliness and wickedness of men who by their wickedness

suppress the truth. [19]For what can be known about God is plain to them, because God has shown it to them. [20]Ever since the creation of the world his invisible nature, namely, his eternal power and deity, has been clearly perceived in the things that have been made. So they are without excuse; [21]for although they knew God they did not honour him as God or give thanks to him, but they became futile in their thinking and their senseless minds were darkened. [22]Claiming to be wise, they became fools, [23]and exchanged the glory of the immortal God for images resembling mortal man or birds or animals or reptiles.

Before developing more particularly the contents of Christ's Gospel, the apostle raises the question of who it is who is to receive it. It is the man without God, the godless person. Without the grace of Christ, man is indeed a godless creature in the sense that he opposes God's truth in his actions and thoughts, and is therefore also denying to his fellowman his right. Yet he is not a godless creature in the sense that he gets rid of God in general. Man is always under the power of God, either of his grace or his wrath. God's wrath is the "adverse wind" of the divine will which he comes to feel who runs into it. God also reveals his nearness to the godless creature precisely in his wrath, thereby declaring that he is not mocked.

Thus there is no human existence without a relation to God. The pagan religions testify of this, too. They would not exist if God did not at first and inescapably declare himself to everyone since the dawn of humanity in his works, in nature and history. The denial of such a "general revelation" preceding the historical revelation of grace in Jesus Christ can appeal neither to Paul nor to the Bible at large. It contradicts the fact of responsibility. If man did not know God, how could he be responsible? But he is responsible, for he knows about God on the strength of the divine self-revelation. The apostle does not speak of a past, now buried, possibility but of something actually present; for it is true of everyone that he is inexcusable in his godlessness. It is true of every godless man that he does not give the honour to the God who made himself known to him, but obscures the divine revelation by the productions of his own undisciplined imagination and arbitrariness. Man cannot excuse himself by pleading that he could not know God prior to his revelation in Jesus Christ; he could very well know him, namely his majesty as Creator and therefore also the fact that he belongs to God. It is his selfishness, however, which prevents this knowledge from becoming practically effective. He does not want to submit and has no intention of being grateful. Thus the pagan religious world originates as the result of God's revelation and man's sin. Its distinctive mark is image-worship, the failure to distinguish between Creator and creature, the darkening of man's innermost being by his cutting himself loose from God.

This is the exchange by which man in his presumption has made of himself a fool and a madman.

²⁴Therefore God gave them up in the lusts of their hearts to impurity, to the dishonouring of their bodies among themselves, ²⁵because they exchanged the truth about God for a lie and worshipped and served the creature rather than the Creator, who is blessed forever! Amen.

²⁶For this reason God gave them up to dishonourable passions. Their women exchanged natural relations for unnatural, ²⁷and the men likewise gave up natural relations with women and were consumed with passion for one another, men committing shameless acts with men and receiving in their own persons the due penalty for their error.

²⁸And since they did not see fit to acknowledge God, God gave them up to a base mind and to improper conduct. ²⁹They were filled with all manner of wickedness, evil, covetousness, malice. Full of envy, murder, strife, deceit, malignity, they are gossips, ³⁰slanderers, haters of God, insolent, haughty, boastful, inventors of evil, disobedient to parents, ³¹foolish, faithless, heartless, ruthless.

³²Though they know God's decree that those who do such things deserve to die, they not only do them, but approve those who practice them.

The original perversion of man's relationship to God is followed by the perversion of all human relationships. This happens by God's will, it is the effect of his wrath. The basic relationship among men is that of the sexes. For in that way God gives every man his life. Thus the perversion of the divine relationship is especially recognizable in the perversion of the sexual relations. The apostle calls things by their names. Missionary earnestness is incompatible with prudery. But the unmasking of sexual sins is followed by the total picture of the destroyed human fellowship. The result of the stock-taking runs: Man knows indeed the divine command, just as he knows of God from the revelation of his works, yet he takes no notice of it but lives and loves in opposition to God's order. That is the fatal "exchange" which out of what God has created makes that which is sinful and which gives the real life of man its character. Just as the honouring of the Creator is the proper and highest meaning of life, so the idolatrous dishonouring of the Creator and the unnatural, inhuman violation of his creation is the horrible paradox into which man has fallen.

GOD'S WRATH AND JUDGMENT ON JEWS AND GENTILES (2: 1-29)

[1]Therefore you have no excuse, O man, whoever you are, when you judge another; for in passing judgment upon him you condemn yourself, because you, the judge, are doing the very same things. [2]We know that the judgment of God rightly falls upon those who do such things. [3]Do you suppose, O man, that when you judge those who do such things and yet do them yourself, you will escape the judgment of God? [4]Or do you presume upon the riches of his kindness and forbearance and patience? Do you not know that God's kindness is meant to lead you to repentance? [5]But by your hard and impenitent heart you are storing up wrath for yourself on the day of wrath when God's righteous judgment will be revealed. [6]For he will render to every man according to his works: [7]to those who by patience in well-doing seek for glory and honour and immortality, he will give eternal life; [8]but for those who are factious and do not obey the truth, but obey wickedness, there will be wrath and fury. [9]There will be tribulation and distress for every human being who does evil, the Jew first and also the Greek, [10]but glory and honour and peace for every one who does good, the Jew first and also the Greek. [11]For God shows no partiality.

Is not the picture drawn in the first chapter a caricature of humanity? Are there not also, besides those who sink into evil and delight in it, others who by their indignation separate themselves from evil? Yes, if they only did this! For in reality they themselves participate in evil which they perceive and condemn so severely in others. The knowledge of the good is not the good itself. Paul is now thinking—especially, yet not exclusively—of the Jews. Their better knowledge of God's will allows them to believe that they themselves are better and that they will therefore escape God's judgment of wrath. But God never asks about knowledge but about action. He does not ask Christians about their knowledge, but their action; not even a Christian knowledge will help on the day of judgment; for when a man is judged the decision depends exclusively on what he has done. There is, therefore, the difference between those who stand on the day of judgment and those who fail when God will judge according to the action.

What is said here in the second chapter is not revoked later on. At the day of divine judgment actions are decisive. This does not stand in opposition to the doctrine of grace and faith developed in the subsequent chapters but is, on the contrary, at one with it. The question is not whether the doing of good is decisive, but whether one arrives at the doing of good by one's own strength. The curse of moralism is not the fact that the action is being undertaken seriously, but the self-deception of the unredeemed man who regards the action as done in his own strength. That he confuses his knowledge of the good with the doing of the good—this is what makes him untruthful; the Pharisaism of correct doctrine, the hypocrisy which mistakes the idea for the reality.

It is brought to the surface at the divine judgment; nothing stands on the day of judgment except the reality of the good. That this is simply the gift of God is proved by the continuation of the epistle. The day of judgment reveals what is good and what is evil; thus responsibility is ultimately the same as having to give an account of oneself before God. The thought of the judgment debases the good will only when prospect of reward and fear of punishment determine the action. There can be no question of this here; the thought of judgment is not the motivation for the action, yet it secures to the action its eternal gravity. But much has still to be said concerning the real reason for the action.

¹²All who have sinned without the law will also perish without the law, and all who have sinned under the law will be judged by the law. ¹³For it is not the hearers of the law who are righteous before God, but the doers of the law who will be justified. ¹⁴When Gentiles who have not the law do by nature what the law requires, they are a law to themselves, even though they do not have the law. ¹⁵They show that what the law requires is written on their hearts, while their conscience also bears witness and their conflicting thoughts accuse or perhaps excuse them ¹⁶on that day when, according to my gospel, God judges the secrets of men by Christ Jesus.

"Lawless", being without the Law; this is the presumptuous Jewish description of the Gentile. But Paul destroys this presumption of the Jew who possesses the Law. It is not the possession of the Law which decides, but quite simply action. God's revelation is not given in order that one should know it, but that through it He may become the Lord. Thus the absence of the Law among the Gentiles is not the deciding fact. The same truth which was previously expressed as a prohibition is now put in the affirmative: if there are Gentiles who do what is commanded in the Law, then they too will be acknowledged for it on the day of judgment. The knowledge of the divine will has not been withheld from them; it follows upon every revelation of God in which the Creator shows himself to each one, so that no one can excuse himself by saying he has never been able to know the will of God. It has already, however, been said of them that "they know the decree of God" (1 : 32). There is a law written in the heart; in their God-created natural disposition they are a law unto themselves.

Paul here takes up the then current idea of the "natural law", but immediately connects it with his thought of creation. God has written his law into everyone's heart; everyone knows something of right and wrong, good and evil. Thus there also exists a conscience, which according to that secret rule judges the action, consenting or rejecting. But how things are in actual fact will be revealed at the judgment which Jesus Christ will carry out at the last day. Until then, what was true in that accusing and excusing remains hidden. Paul expressly declares that this doctrine of judgment belongs to the message of salvation with which he has been commissioned.

¹⁷But if you call yourself a Jew and rely upon the law and boast of your relation to God ¹⁸and know his will and approve what is excellent, because you are instructed in the law, ¹⁹and if you are sure that you are a guide to the blind, a light to those who are in darkness, ²⁰a corrector of the foolish, a teacher of children, having in the law the embodiment of knowledge and truth—²¹you then who teach others, will you not teach yourself? While you preach against stealing, do you steal? ²²You who say that one must not commit adultery, do you commit adultery? You who abhor idols, do you rob temples? ²³You who boast in the law, do you dishonour God by breaking the law? ²⁴For, as it is written, "The name of God is blasphemed among the Gentiles because of you."

²⁵Circumcision indeed is of value if you obey the law; but if you break the law, your circumcision becomes uncircumcision. ²⁶So, if a man who is uncircumcised keeps the precepts of the law, will not his uncircumcision be regarded as circumcision? ²⁷Then those who are physically uncircumcised but keep the law will condemn you who have the written code and circumcision but break the law. ²⁸For he is not a real Jew who is one outwardly, nor is true circumcision something external and physical. ²⁹He is a Jew who is one inwardly, and real circumcision is a matter of the heart, spiritual and not literal. His praise is not from men but from God.

Previously Paul has explicitly addressed himself to the law-less Gentiles. He now turns to the Jews who know the Law; whose ways of thinking he knew well, of course, from his own days of Pharisaism. He knows the proud feeling of the man who possesses and understands the God-given Law, the consciousness of superiority of him who has been instructed in it from his youth, who is therefore called to be a teacher and leader. But this knowing better must prove itself in action; if he does not do it then it has repercussions on the possessor and makes him all the guiltier.

Since becoming a disciple of Christ, Paul knows that all mere orthodoxy, all mere knowledge concerning God's will, is not only nothing but less than nothing. The more knowledge, the more obligation. The maintaining of revealed doctrine becomes blasphemy if it is not borne out by the corresponding testimony of the life. He who is always appealing to the word of God without his life and conduct corresponding to this knowledge of God, dishonours God's name, making him an object of mockery and hatred. It is just those who know so well how to talk about God who make his name hateful among men, because their lives darken the picture of God and turn it into a caricature. The Lord is judged by the life of his servants, and this is truer the more zealously they appeal to him. The life of this people of God does not arouse desire in the world to know this God and to belong to him. The result of their enterprises of conversion is an absolute negative.

Yet do they not, after all, have the written word and the sacrament of circumcision? Have they not proved themselves to be God's people by this double possession? Certain as it is that it is something tremendous to be called by God in this way, they do not become thereby God's people. One is not a real "Jew", someone truly belonging to God, because of the external marks as such, but by the spiritual reality. Just as it is not the knowing of God's will which avails before God's judgment but solely the doing of his will, so it is also not the fact of having been circumcised, the external receiving of the sacrament, which determines one's membership of God's people, but that which has become real in the heart, at the centre of the person, in the life dependent on God. "Wherever God's Word may be preached, his precepts remain a letter and dead words so long as they are not received by men with a pure heart; only where they pierce to the soul do they become, so to speak, changed into Spirit" (Calvin). Membership badges without loyalty and obedience are of no value. Attachment to the Church without discipleship is the husk without the kernel.

Does everything therefore depend on the practical life and not on religion? Rightly understood, yes. Yet not in the way a moralism of the Enlightenment understands it. In reality it is only a question of the "practical life", the doing of good. But who really does what is good? Where are the men, Jews and Gentiles, who can stand before the claim of the divine law, who at God's judgment might hope for a favourable verdict in accordance with their deeds? The right kind of doing good is the same as true religion, namely the life of the person, of the heart, from and in the Word of God—which is the same as life in the Holy Spirit. Where this happens, then everything

23

is well with man and his relationship to God, just as God wants
it to be. Man in that position is such that God can praise him:
"Well done, good and faithful servant, enter into the joy of
your master." But where is this man?

THE PRIVILEGE OF THE JEWS NO EXCUSE (3: 1-8)

¹Then what advantage has the Jew? Or what is the value of
circumcision? ²Much in every way. To begin with, the Jews are
entrusted with the oracles of God. ³What if some were unfaithful? Does their faithlessness nullify the faithfulness of God?
⁴By no means! Let God be true though every man be false, as it
is written,
> "That thou mayest be justified in thy words,
>   and prevail when thou art judged."

In the previous chapter Paul destroyed the false presumption
of the pious Pharisee who considered himself superior to the
rest of mankind and exempted from Divine judgment by his
knowledge of God's revealed will and the sign of the divine
covenant ratified on him. Neither offers any protection against
God's righteous judgment. Man cannot hide himself from God's
demand either behind his theological and biblical knowledge
or his Church membership and his participation in its sacraments. Where the ultimate question concerns the saving or
damning relationship to God, other standards apply. But
this does not mean that what the Jew actually possesses is
meaningless. The difference between him and the others is
indeed a tremendous one; for he has been entrusted with
God's Word of revelation. To dispute this superiority, which
makes Israel the chosen people, would never occur to Paul.

It has pleased God to make Israel the custodian of the divine
treasure of revelation. No one can contend with Israel for this
special rank in the history of mankind. Israel has the Bible,
and the Bible is the fountain of revelation; whoever drinks from
it is healed. This gift of God is independent of what the Jewish
people, to whom it was first given, do with it. The Gospel
remains God's word however corrupt may be the Church that
offers it. God's truth shines only the brighter against the dark
background of the human lie. God's fidelity is greater than
man's faithlessness. Yes, it is in the light of the fidelity and truth

of God that we first see how deeply all humanity is entangled in unfaithfulness.

> [5]But if our wickedness serves to show the justice of God, what shall we say? That God is unjust to inflict wrath on us? (I speak in a human way.) [6]By no means! For then how could God judge the world? [7]But if through my falsehood God's truthfulness abounds to his glory, why am I still being condemned as a sinner? [8]And why not do evil that good may come?—as some people slanderously charge us with saying. Their condemnation is just.

It is part of God's incomprehensibly wise government of the world that he can also use man's evil doings for the purpose of his kingdom, which is the essence of everything that is good. He who used the betrayal of Judas as a means for revealing his saving faithfulness can also, as Paul will demonstrate still more clearly in the eleventh chapter, include Israel's disobedience in the fabric of the history of redemption (*Heilsgeschichte*). Men's sinfulness constitutes no hindrance to God. But shortsighted, frivolous men stumble over this most profound truth, inferring from it that sin is not contrary to God. Since they do not want to accept the message of God's unlimited grace, they attribute to its proclaimer the blasphemous doctrine that one should quietly continue to sin, for thereby one only illuminates God's greatness the more. Like this one can, by giving free rein to human logic, make a dreadful heresy out of any biblical truth. What we ought or ought not to do is one thing; what God is able to make of our wrong is another. The one, like the other, results from God taking it seriously; but human capacity of thought can never deal with it. God is the judge of every wrong; yet he is also the one who can bring good out of evil. The two things ought to remain unconfused; they both hold true, whatever our logic may do with them.

And now Paul has reached the stage where he can strike the decisive blow against every kind of human presumption, so that he may crush it before going on to speak of what the whole letter points to: God's gracious act of reconciliation in Jesus Christ.

GOD'S JUDGMENT ON SINFUL HUMANITY (3: 9-20)

⁹What then? Are we Jews any better off? No, not at all; for I have already charged that all men, both Jews and Greeks, are under the power of sin, ¹⁰as it is written:

"None is righteous, no, not one;
¹¹no one understands, no one seeks for God.
¹²All have turned aside, together they have gone wrong;
no one does good, not even one."
¹³"Their throat is an open grave,
they use their tongues to deceive."
"The venom of asps is under their lips."
¹⁴"Their mouth is full of curses and bitterness."
¹⁵"Their feet are swift to shed blood,
¹⁶in their paths are ruin and misery,
¹⁷and the way of peace they do not know."
¹⁸"There is no fear of God before their eyes."

¹⁹Now we know that whatever the law says it speaks to those who are under the law, so that every mouth may be stopped, and the whole world may be held accountable to God. ²⁰For no human being will be justified in his sight by works of the law since through the law comes knowledge of sin.

The Jews and Greeks, those who know the revealed will of God from Holy Scripture and those who do not know it, the elect to whom has been entrusted the holy treasure of God's word, who from their youth have been made familiar with it, and all the rest who do not possess this advantage—they all live "under the power of sin". This is the common denominator of all, however great the differences may be in other respects. The difference between the people of God and the others is great and ought not to be denied; but it is nothing when the question is raised: What about the last and decisive thing? How will you appear then, before God's judgment? The verdict then can only run: Guilty. We have to expect absolute condemnation. This terrible verdict concerns all in so far as they appeal to the Law, in so far as they wish to appear in their own righteousness.

Much still remains to be said about what "under the law" means. Meantime the final result is simply announced: Whoever wants to place himself opposite God on the ground of the Law as the one who is to fulfil God's demand in his own

strength, must now hear what his prospects are. His condemnation is certain.

Paul no longer demonstrates this from experience. He has
already done so in the first and second chapters. Here it is
sufficient for him to cite the verdict, of the Old Testament
Scriptures. One thing is said in different ways: If one goes to
the heart of the matter, then man, every man, is in a bad way.
The façade may look more or less magnificent—even Paul does
not overlook the difference between decent people and riff-raff
—yet the inner state is the same: Godlessness. There are "moving staircases" in the undergrounds of our great cities which
move downwards whether one stands still or is walking on them.
Whoever happens to stand on these stairs is on the downward
move even though he is trying to walk up. The same is true of
those who live "under the law". To be sure, there are a thousand possibilities here of going up and down, differences which
in their place may be quite noticeable. But it alters nothing as
to the general direction. It goes down irresistibly towards the
judgment. Once one stands opposite God on the ground of the
Law—God demands of man that he shall fulfil his command—
then the direction is fixed; godlessness is present in spite of
every kind of moral or religious exertion. Why this is so we shall
hear later. The question we are concerned with here is: Is there
then no other possibility, no other "ground" on which we are
able to stand?

Before giving an answer to this main question we must first
remove the misunderstanding that the Law itself was to blame
for this dreadful position of man. The Law, God's command,
cannot help us once sin is present. It is the delusion of moralism,
even of religiously "deepened" moralism, that man can
extricate himself from sin by treating God's command seriously
in practice, climbing up it, as it were. The following chapters
will thoroughly destroy this delusion. Yet this does not mean
that no importance at all is to be attached to God's Law on
the path of salvation by which God leads us. The Law cannot
make us righteous, but it can reveal to us what is wrong.
Through the Law comes the knowledge of sin. This is no small
matter. If there still had to be something other than the way
of the Law, we do not bypass the Law to reach this other thing
but only go right through the Law. The Law, taken seriously,

breaks the arrogance of man; yes, it breaks man himself. But
only as someone who is broken, as a person who is thoroughly
shaken, as someone who has come to the end of his tether, can
he understand what has to be said to him now as being the
one and all of the Gospel message.

B. THE REDEMPTION THROUGH JESUS CHRIST
(3: 21—8: 39)

THE NEW BASIS OF LIFE, THE GIFT
OF RIGHTEOUSNESS (3: 21-31)

[21]But now the righteousness of God has been manifested
apart from law, although the law and the prophets bear
witness to it, [22]the righteousness of God through faith in Jesus
Christ for all who believe. For there is no distinction; [23]since
all have sinned and fall short of the glory of God, [24]they are
justified by his grace as a gift, through the redemption which is
in Christ Jesus, [25]whom God put forward as an expiation by his
blood, to be received by faith. This was to show God's righteousness, because in his divine forbearance he had passed over
former sins; [26]it was to prove at the present time that he himself
is righteous and that he justifies him who has faith in Jesus.

[27]Then what becomes of our boasting? It is excluded. On
what principle? On the principle of works? No, but on the
principle of faith. [28]For we hold that a man is justified by
faith apart from works of law. [29]Or is God the God of Jews only?
Is he not the God of Gentiles also? Yes, of Gentiles also, [30]since
God is one; and he will justify the circumcised on the ground
of their faith and the uncircumcised because of their faith.
[31]Do we then overthrow the law by this faith? By no means!
On the contrary, we uphold the law.

"The knowledge of sin"; that was the conclusion of the first
introductory part of the letter. Whether Jew or Gentile,
whether partaking of the divine instruction or not, whether
with or without the law, all are under sin. However vast the
differences among men may otherwise be, this at any rate
they have all in common. All live "down in the dark" and
therefore in night (13: 12). "But now—"—that there is this
"but now"—this is the glad tidings, this is the content of

the proclamation by the apostles, the very thing which makes Paul a debtor both to the Jews and the Gentiles, leading him from country to country and even to Rome, that "power of God for the salvation of all who believe". "But now" everything has become new, the life "down in the dark" has ended, the day of God has dawned upon mankind.

The turning-point in world history has come. It is not a new knowledge, a new way, a new religion or philosophy or ethics which has been found, but God Himself has stepped out of his concealment, thereby radically changing the condition of mankind. The righteousness of God has broken forth, the life of God Himself, the love of God which is the only absolute right, the right that is divine.

This has happened "apart", in separation, from the Law. The Law too is from God but the Law is not God Himself. We may re-write this first sentence of the new section: But now, after men have in vain sought God in their own way, God Himself has entered into their midst and made known to them his way and his life. Where the Law is, then the question concerns man's doings, man's righteousness. But grace means that now the question relates to the actions of God and his righteousness, and therefore to how God is setting the world right. This is not something entirely new, for God's witnesses of the Old Covenant have spoken of it; it is the theme of the Old Testament, the "Law and the Prophets". But that which was only proclaimed by them has now happened and become visible in Jesus Christ.

Since it is as a man, however, that God thus appears as he is himself, in his own righteousness, so it is also the existence and life of men which becomes different by this appearing of God. It ought to become "righteous". God's nature as the prophets perceived it and as it was revealed in Jesus Christ is to be seen in just this, that he communicates himself, that he lets man share in his life. His righteousness therefore is that which men ought to receive, and which they all do receive inasmuch as they believe. They themselves are, of course, not "righteous", for we know that they are sinners without exception. They lack the one thing which alone could make them righteous: the righteousness of God, the splendour, the glory of the divine life. That they are sinners and that they lack this glorious life of God is obviously one and the same thing. They just live "down in the dark", not in the divine sunshine. This has now been changed. God has done the thing whereby men come to share in what they lack; namely, God's righteousness. How does this impossible thing happen?

It happens through God removing that which separates men from himself, that is, guilt, and acknowledging those who were no longer his own as his own. He justifies the unrighteous, he grants to them what they do not have, which they have lost to all eternity: his unconditioned love. He says to them the opposite of what he should have said to them had he wished to judge them according to the Law: You are righteous in my sight. He receives them, the apostates, into his fellowship. Why? Because he wishes to. On what basis? Purely in the form of a gift, on the basis of his grace. God therefore treats sin simply as if it were nothing, simply passing it over? Quite the contrary. This grace, which indeed costs man nothing, costs God his Son. He let Jesus Christ die as a proof of his righteousness, so that forgiveness is not going to be misunderstood as a passing-over of guilt.

It is not as if God would have to be appeased first before he were able to turn his love towards men; neither the letter to the Romans nor the rest of the New Testament knows of a reconciliation whose object is God. Jesus truly is the reconciler —"the means of reconciliation"—"the ark of the covenant" (strictly: the cover of the ark of the covenant) as Paul calls him in reference to the Israelite custom of sacrificial atonement; but the performer of this reconciliation is solely God. It does not happen for God's sake but for man's. Otherwise it would not become manifest that God's righteousness is also one that judges and punishes, since his forgiveness would be mistaken for a mere overlooking of sin. Christ's death is the sign of judging righteousness, as well as of forgiving love; of God's wrath "upon every kind of godlessness and unrighteousness of men" as well as that of his incomprehensible mercy. The blood of Christ serves not for the removal but for the revelation of his punitive wrath on sins. The divine love is not the effect but the cause of the act of reconciliation.

God's righteousness wishes to communicate itself to man as it has already communicated itself to mankind in Jesus Christ.

But how does this happen? How does man receive what belongs to God? Through faith; that is, by man receiving what God gives to him. Faith means here, where it is a question of God's justification of the sinner, man's trusting what God says to him although it goes against all his own experience, turning upside down all his customary ideas of right and wrong. The sinner is righteous. In what way? Because God declares it to be so. But how can God say what is not really true at all? Surely, the sinner is not a righteous man? It is so because righteousness is not something that man can have "of himself", since righteousness is what man receives from God and in fact through God's bestowing declaration. When God declares: You are righteous in my sight, you are my beloved son in whom I am well pleased; then man in believing this is no longer the same man as he was before but precisely a new person, the beloved son. We shall have more to say about this.

Yet this much is already clear and beyond doubt: this righteousness is not one which has been gained, but bestowed. Here things have happened differently from where man strives to fulfil God's command by himself. Paul once more contrasts the two kinds of righteousness: righteousness through the Law, that is, according to the active way of works, and righteousness by faith. In the Law it is self-activity, man as the producer of righteousness; in faith it is pure receptivity, man as the recipient of the divine gift. This latter is the justified person, the one who is righteous in the true sense of the word. Man's state of righteousness is not one that he has gained for himself but one which is conferred upon him; man's true existence is not independence but dependence upon God. Justification by faith alone is therefore not a kind of divine "as if", but a divine creation. Thus absolutely all "boasting" is excluded; so long as man is intent on his glory he is still living in the sinful misunderstanding of himself. He has still not understood that the only glory which he can have is to realize that he lives entirely by what God has granted to him. Therefore he who glories, let him glory in God.

And the Law? It is not merely Paul, the former Pharisee and Jew, who cannot shake off the question of the Law. Where God's Law disappears from his consciousness man sinks into the morass of contingency and arbitrariness; he can no longer understand the grace of God. To be sure, God is not only the God of the Jews but also of the Gentiles, of those "without the Law", since justification by faith stands above this opposition, and Christ is proclaimed as the Saviour of the Gentiles as well as of the Jews. Both, moreover, can receive their salvation only along the path of faith "apart from the Law". But the Law is not thereby annulled. It is, of course, no longer the ground on which men are standing as those made righteous by faith, yet it still is the rule by which all, even the new righteousness, must prove itself to be such. Here the words of Our Lord are applicable: "For I tell you, unless your righteousness exceeds that of the scribes and Pharisees, you will never enter the kingdom of heaven" (Matt. 5: 20). The better righteousness, the righteousness of faith, cannot undercut the righteousness of the Law. It must prove itself as true righteousness by helping to realization what the Law demands. Thus through the righteousness of faith the Law is not annulled but rather confirmed. How this is to be understood can, however, only be made clear in a later context.

Further, there is another respect in which Paul does not deny his Judaism. The Old Testament is and remains Holy Scripture, and even the New Testament which has come through Jesus Christ must be displayed in its continuity with the teaching of the Old Testament. We have just heard that God's righteousness, the righteousness of faith, is testified by the Old Testament, by the "Law and the Prophets". The aim of the fourth chapter is to prove this, and also to expound further the concept of righteousness by faith.

THE RIGHTEOUSNESS OF FAITH IN
THE OLD AND THE NEW COVENANT (4: 1-25)

[1]What then shall we say about Abraham, our forefather according to the flesh? [2]For if Abraham was justified by works, he has something to boast about, but not before God. [3]For what does the scripture say? "Abraham believed God, and it was reckoned to him as righteousness." [4]Now to one who works, his wages are not reckoned as a gift but as his due. [5]And to one who does not work but trusts him who justifies the ungodly, his faith is reckoned as righteousness. [6]So also David

32

pronounces a blessing upon the man to whom God reckons righteousness apart from works:

⁷"Blessed are those whose iniquities are forgiven, and whose sins are covered;

⁸blessed is the man against whom the Lord will not reckon his sin."

⁹Is this blessing pronounced only upon the circumcised, or also upon the uncircumcised? We say that faith was reckoned to Abraham as righteousness. ¹⁰How then was it reckoned to him? Was it before or after he had been circumcised? It was not after, but before he was circumcised. ¹¹He received circumcision as a sign or seal of the righteousness which he had by faith while he was still uncircumcised. The purpose was to make him the father of all who believe without being circumcised and who thus have righteousness reckoned to them, ¹²and likewise the father of the circumcised who are not merely circumcised but also follow the example of the faith which our father Abraham had before he was circumcised.

Jesus, the Christ, is the Messiah promised in the Old Testament. The history of redemption (*Heilsgeschichte*) does not begin with him but culminates in him. The New Testament cannot be understood without the Old Testament. It is no accident that salvation "comes from the Jews", sure though it is that this salvation, the Saviour, is more than Israel had in its Messianic hope and covenant with God. Paul has to give to the Jews in the Christian Community a special account of how this utterly new thing, which has been given to mankind in Jesus Christ, agrees with the promises made to the fathers, and how the righteousness by faith that Paul proclaims is related to the picture of the truly pious man delivered to the fathers. Does the Old Testament also know something of righteousness by faith?

In Abraham both were combined: the history of redemption which began with the separation of Israel from the nations of the world and what through God's word had been made known to the fathers as the right kind of conduct before God. Abraham was not merely the physical ancestor of Israel but at the same time the prototype of the true believer. When a Jew called himself a son of Abraham, he thought just as much of the responsibility of this inheritance as of the natural descent.

What kind of piety then was Abraham's? "What was it that Abraham, our physical ancestor, had found?" On the answer to this question depended whether the message of Paul was an innovation which stood outside the context of the earlier history of redemption, or whether what was begun in Abraham had been fulfilled by Jesus.

At first, there seems to be a contradiction here. Abraham is known for his piety, hence for his mode of life which is pleasing to God, and hence for "the works of the Law", the fulfilling of God's command. But what is it that is well-pleasing to God in regard to Abraham? What does Scripture emphasize as the decisive thing in him? It is nothing but his faith, his trusting in God, his leaving everything to God and expecting everything from God. And not only that. Scripture expressly states that God imputed his faith to him as righteousness. It was not that Abraham was righteous through his fulfilling of the Law, but that the title "righteous" was bestowed upon him as a gift from God because he believed. One may, of course, also speak of faith as a virtue like others; one could also look upon faith as an "achievement" on the basis of which the title "righteous" belonged to him by right. But that is not the question here. It does not speak about faith alongside other things and thus about a virtue; rather, by exclusively stressing faith is indicated that it is concerned with quite a different relationship to God: Abraham did not wish to be something himself but placed himself entirely in God's hand. Therefore the imputing it to him as righteousness is no mere acknowledgment of a present fact. This man is a righteous person. Why should someone who believes be a righteous man? This imputation is grace.

The second witness to righteousness by faith is David. He too speaks in his Psalms of "imputing", but of non-imputation as well; the non-imputation of guilt. He declares him blessed to whom it happens and whose sin is forgiven. Righteousness by forgiveness is certainly no righteousness of achievement but purely a bestowed righteousness. The forgiveness of sins is, of course, wholly the work of God; man is a mere recipient. He is not a righteous man in himself and of himself but because of what God speaks to him. For the first time Paul uses for righteousness by faith the expression which was familiar to everyone through the Old Testament and to Christians

34

especially through the sayings of the Lord: the forgiveness
of sins.

If the connection with the Old Testament is thus clarified
by definite examples, the opposite question has now to be
answered: Does the declaration to Abraham and David, the
Psalmist, also apply to the Gentiles? Can Abraham be considered as the ancestor of the Gentile Christians as well, whose
physical forefather he certainly is not, and is the righteousness
by forgiveness therefore also meant for the Gentiles? The mark
of the Jews is circumcision. Whoever does not share in circumcision may indeed be a Jew in the purely physical sense, yet
in the spiritual sense of partaking of the promises of the fathers
he is not a Jew. Abraham, however, at the moment when God
reckoned faith to him as righteousness, Abraham the father of
faith, is not a Jew in this sense but a Gentile, so to speak. The
circumcision was only later added as a seal of the righteousness
by faith already bestowed. Why, therefore, should this Abraham, who was righteous by faith as an uncircumcised person
and non-Jew, not have sons who like himself receive the
righteousness by faith without circumcision as a gift? Here
already we catch a glimpse of the theme of Rom. 9. This
righteousness is not tied to any Law, for it is solely the work of
the sovereign rule of God, who elects whom he will. God is
bound to nothing except his own will. For righteousness by
faith is the righteousness of God, his act, his gift; it is free as
God Himself is free. God is also not fettered to his own signs.
Only one condition always stands. It has already been mentioned when the theme of God's righteousness was touched
upon the first time, it was again clearly emphasized when the
reconciling act of Christ was mentioned; fundamentally it is
not a condition but the subject itself seen from the reverse side:
the righteousness of God is righteousness by faith. Only faith
can partake of it. "*To all* who believe"; that always means:
only to those who believe. Thus Abraham too is the father
solely of those who "follow the example of his faith". They
who believe are the righteous; the righteous are those who
believe. The righteousness of God is righteousness by faith.

¹³The promise to Abraham and his descendants, that they
should inherit the world, did not come through the law but

through the righteousness of faith. ¹⁴If it is the adherents of the law who are to be the heirs, faith is null and the promise is void. ¹⁵For the law brings wrath, but where there is no law there is no transgression.

¹⁶That is why it depends on faith, in order that the promise may rest on grace and be guaranteed to all his descendants— not only to the adherents of the law but also to those who share the faith of Abraham, for he is the father of us all, ¹⁷as it is written, "I have made you the father of many nations"— in the presence of the God in whom he believed, who gives life to the dead and calls into existence the things that do not exist. ¹⁸In hope he believed against hope, that he should become the father of many nations; as he had been told, "So shall your descendants be." ¹⁹He did not weaken in faith when he considered his own body, which was as good as dead because he was about a hundred years old, or when he considered the barrenness of Sarah's womb. ²⁰No distrust made him waver concerning the promise of God, but he grew strong in his faith as he gave glory to God, ²¹fully convinced that God was able to do what he had promised. ²²That is why his faith was "reckoned to him as righteousness." ²³But the words, "it was reckoned to him," were written not for his sake alone, ²⁴but for ours also. It will be reckoned to us who believe in him that raised from the dead Jesus our Lord, ²⁵who was put to death for our trespasses and raised for our justification.

Righteousness by faith, hence, the message of the transformation of all things through God's intervention in Jesus Christ, does not stand outside the context of the history of redemption which the Old Testament declares to us. Rather, that which was given through Christ shows itself as the fulfilment of what Abraham had already received. Is there ultimately then nothing in the opposition between law and faith? As in his letter to the Galatians, so also here Paul has to fight on two fronts. Not without the Old Testament! But not with the Law! Just as he differentiated in his epistle to the Galatians between the two sides of the Old Covenant: the covenant of the Law (the Jewish Jerusalem, Hagar, Sinai) and the covenant of Promise (Sarah, the Jerusalem above), so here too he draws a sharp distinction between Law and Promise in regard to Abraham's inheritance. For the question can never be whether the Law is or is not from God. That is certain. The question can only be—and this is the all-decisive question—whether righteousness comes from the Law or not. It is as important for Paul to destroy every link between the righteousness of the Law and the righteousness by faith as it is for him not to snap the thread between the Old and the New Covenant. Here there is ño Both—And. Here there is only the keen unconditional either—or.

For the question here is whether man becomes "righteous" of himself or through the gift of God. If that inheritance can be obtained also along the path of the Law, then faith is done for, then faith is not faith and promise not promise; then Jesus Christ is not the Saviour for all nor is he the one apart from whom there is no salvation. Here, therefore, absolutely everything is being decided; everything is at stake in the message of the apostle, and not only in his message but in that of all apostles, in the message about Jesus Christ, the Messiah. But at the same time it concerns the question whether one must be a Jew in order to partake of salvation or whether salvation is for all. If salvation is tied to the Law, then the Jews are right: one must be a Jew in order to partake of it. Then Abraham is certainly not the father of all nations. Yet he is that, because he is the father of those who believe, of those who do not rely on their own achievement but look for everything from the activity of God.

If Paul has previously talked in the abstract, so to speak, of the faith of Abraham, he is now showing us what Abraham believed. Abraham believed in the impossible, in that which is contrary to all human expectation. As the existence of genuine love shows itself especially when we are concerned with loving our enemy, so the existence of faith in God's promise is completely clear only where God's promise runs counter to human expectation and calculation. Whether one really relies on God's word alone becomes manifest only where God's word is not supported by any rational basis, but where, on the contrary, it is opposed to what one must consider probable on the basis of reason.

God's promise to Abraham was of that kind. Humanly speaking, it was impossible for him to have descendants, and hence to become the father of many nations. Abraham was no visionary. He knew what being old means in this case, he

37

knew what a dead womb means for the question of posterity. He thus knew that, humanly, nothing was to be expected. What did he do, then? He counted on God's truthfulness and on God's wonderful power. God's word meant more to him than experience. He not only felt but acknowledged and affirmed his entire dependence upon God. This really is to believe. By this act of believing man surrenders himself and reckons only with God; therefore God exerts his influence in this faith, indeed, God asserts himself in this faith. Thus this faith is reckoned as righteousness not because it is a record achievement, a virtue outshining all other virtues, a supernatural virtue, but quite simply because, in this act of believing, man gives God his place.

Here stands out clearly not only the nature of faith but also the nature of God. The true understanding of God corresponds to true faith. God is the absolute Lord, the sovereign Creator. That kind of absolute faith can exist only towards this God. To know oneself absolutely dependent on God, to surrender oneself unconditionally into his hand, expecting everything from him, can only happen if God is the one who is all-powerful, who has the absolute power of disposal, for whose will there exists no limit and no hindrance. This is the God who calls into being that which is not. Just as he calls him who is not righteous, but a sinner, into righteousness—his word is creative power—so he calls into existence that which is not. Only from such a God could Abraham expect the realization of that promise; only because by faith he recognized him as such could he expect from him this impossible thing; new life coming from what was dead, a posterity from Sarah's dead womb, numerous as the stars of heaven. This faith became righteousness because in it God was acknowledged and honoured in his true divinity. This faith is nothing less than God's influence exerting itself upon man, in man. Only through such a faith does God truly become the Lord of man.

Thus this righteousness by faith is also not bound by any limits. Where one believes in this way, there God is honoured as he desires to be honoured; there all other conditions are irrelevant. The faith of the Christian Community is indeed also of this sort. Where one believes in this God with this faith, there the distinction between Jew and non-Jew loses every meaning. In Christ "is neither Jew nor Greek"; they are "all one" (Gal. 3: 28). For it is faith in the God who has shown himself in the raising of Jesus from the dead as the absolute Lord; it is a faith which trusts God in everything by trusting him in this. By the death and resurrection of Jesus Christ the same absolute power is effectual. In unlimited freedom over his own Law God allows the righteous to suffer for the un-righteous; in sovereign loving power he transmits the righteous-ness of the Son, which is his own, to us sinners; in absolute creative power he changes the death of Christ into the victory of his life for mankind.

Thus Abraham's faith is present and has reached its fulfil-ment in Christ's Community. Only in Jesus Christ does that inheritance in which Abraham believed become a reality; for only through him, by his atoning death and victory over death and the grave, are all nations included in the history of redemp-tion that began with Abraham and the setting apart of Israel. And only the resurrection of Jesus from the dead, which is the centre of the message about Christ, makes manifest the meaning of God creating life out of death. What Abraham has experi-enced is indeed a beginning, but yet only a beginning of what Christ's Community experiences in the realization of the divine promise of inheritance.

In this way the apostle, looking back from Christ, reads his Old Testament, his Bible, with its promises. He sees the unity between what was given to the fathers and what to us in Jesus Christ; yet he also perceives the difference, which consists in just this: that the true meaning of what was then promised and believed is only emerging now. We are not always able to · follow the apostle in detail in his scriptural expositions, which frequently reflect his former connection with the rabbinic method of scriptural interpretation. Yet his total view must be shared by us. The meaning of the Old Testament is fulfilled only by Jesus Christ. With its hope for the Messiah and expec-tation of the new Covenant, it points clearly enough beyond itself. The Old Testament contains the seed which has reached its full blossom in the New Testament. The Old Testament portrays in a preliminary way what gained its final form in the New Testament, just as the prophets are the forerunners of the Messiah and not the Messiah himself. God has not given us from above a ready-made book of revelation, but he began with mankind a history whose testimonies have been given to us in the Old Testament and in which, thanks to this witness, we share. But this history from the very beginning is "directed" towards Jesus Christ, and its meaning therefore can be understood only through him. He himself is its meaning, so surely as it is the one God who has unveiled Himself to us and made his covenant with mankind imperfectly in the words of the prophets and perfectly in Jesus Christ.

THE NEW PROSPECT (5: 1-11)

[1]Therefore, since we are justified by faith, we have peace with God through our Lord Jesus Christ. [2]Through him we have obtained access to this grace in which we stand, and we rejoice in our hope of sharing the glory of God. [3]More than that, we rejoice in our sufferings, knowing that suffering produces endurance, [4]and endurance produces character, and character produces hope, [5]and hope does not disappoint us, because God's love has been poured into our hearts through the Holy Spirit which has been given to us.

[6]While we were yet helpless, at the right time Christ died for the ungodly. [7]Why, one will hardly die for a righteous man—though perhaps for a good man one will dare even to die. [8]But God shows his love for us in that while we were yet sinners Christ died for us. [9]Since, therefore, we are now justified by his blood, much more shall we be saved by him from the wrath of God. [10]For if while we were enemies we were reconciled to God by the death of his Son, much more, now that we are reconciled, shall we be saved by his life. [11]Not only so, but we also rejoice in God through our Lord Jesus Christ, through whom we have now received our reconciliation.

A new basis of life has been laid through Jesus Christ. We no longer stand on the ground of the Law, i.e., of our own deeds, but on the ground of God's action. We have now a new position, the Christ-position or the Christian position. What is implied by living in this position?

The first thing is: We "stand" differently towards God now. Before, there was a state of war, enmity; now peace has come. Between God and us things previously were bad; now all is well. We need no longer as before vainly trouble ourselves to set

right our relationship with God. It has been settled by himself.
We are no longer under wrath, but in grace. We have free
access to God. The bad conscience which otherwise would
always scare us away from God has been silenced. It is not
because we have set ourselves right in such a way that the bad
conscience found nothing else of which to accuse us, but
because Christ has put this terrible watchman into chains
before God's holy throne and silenced him. We may now
associate with God, go in and out before him, as it were, as sons
in the house of their father. Of course, we are as yet not in that
perfect communion with God which is called "seeing face to
face". We are still "on earth" and God is "in heaven"; we are
here still in a very earthly and fragile life and not yet in glory.
But we know that that glory is ours. We are not yet at home,
but we are on our way there and we know that we shall reach
the goal, the only goal, which may be called the end, the glory
of God, life eternal. The certainty that this goal is ours is our
hope, and whoever has this hope is full of cheer, like someone
on the point of taking possession of a rich inheritance.

Full of cheer in the midst of the vexations of this age, this
bad course of the world. Yes, even these vexations and grievous
experiences must themselves serve the purpose of strengthening
that cheerful spirit. Opposition makes for strength, persever-
ance and steadfastness. It now proves that faith is no imagination but really "the power of God". The new position proves
itself as new life. One notices that things have really become
different, that one can master the difficulties of every day in a
different manner from before. And this experience allows hope
to gleam more brightly: What God has so mightily begun, that
he will complete too. Whoever experiences the power of Christ
in the present so clearly, for him the issue of the struggle, the
final goal of the long way, cannot be in doubt.

The most important experience, however, is that "God's love
has been poured into our hearts through the Holy Spirit".
We not only believe this, it is now also an experience. That is
exactly the meaning of "poured into our hearts". The experience of the present power of God's love has now also been
granted to us, not without faith nor independently of faith but
through faith. Through faith in God's love in Jesus Christ, this
same love is now also shared by us, making itself felt as a real

power of life. "The abundant revelation of God's love flows through our whole heart. It penetrates every corner and does not only alleviate sadness: it mixes itself like a mild seasoning with all trials, lending them a pleasant flavour" (Calvin). Luther, like Augustine, understood the "love of God" as "love towards God". The argument as to whether this is correct is surely an idle one. For where God's love really becomes an experience it is at the same time and without more ado also love towards God. Love, after all, can only be accepted if it is given in return. Whoever perceives the love of God also loves God. "Therefore God's love alone, which is the purest feeling towards God, setting right the heart, removes unrighteousness; it alone destroys the satisfaction of one's own righteousness. For it loves God Himself only and solely, not just God's gifts" (Luther). This experience of God's love is the experience of the Holy Spirit, which Paul calls the pledge of hope.

But at once our view must be turned away again from what happens in us towards Christ Himself, the "Christ for us". For he is the fountain of this love and only by our looking to him does this fountain flow. The Christian position is not something by itself but precisely our being in Christ. We must make clear to ourselves the unheard-of event of Christ's sacrifice if we are to become fully certain of the incomprehensible love of God and with it of the glorious final goal.

Paul can hardly express this unheard-of thing. He wrestles with the language, and keeps on beginning all over again. The death of the righteous man on behalf of sinners is something quite inconceivable. Yet therein God proves his love, which exceeds all our powers of imagination. Christ and God are for Paul so much of a unity that for him the self-sacrifice of the Son is simply the proof of the Father's love. If once we have reached the certainty that God has given himself in Jesus Christ for us, the godless, then no doubt can arise in us regarding the future. This past unequivocally means salvation, complete redemption as to the future. More, this past already includes that future in the same way as the beginning of a sentence already contains the end of it. It is one "stroke" of God's hand. Reconciliation is already the beginning of salvation and must fulfil itself in salvation. Once again it becomes clear here that it is not God who becomes reconciled, but we who become reconciled to God; for it is God who does everything. Yet all this does indeed concern our deliverance from his wrath through his love. For there exist only these two possibilities: being under God's wrath and being in God's love. But God wills—this is his love towards us sinners—that we move out of the realm of wrath into the sphere of his love. Of course, he also loves the sinners, towards whom he must show wrath so long as they do not trust his love. That they, that we, may trust his love, He has sacrificed his own Son for us.

THE HISTORY OF DEATH AND THE HISTORY OF LIFE (5: 12-21)

[12]Therefore as sin came into the world through one man and death through sin, and so death spread to all men because all men sinned—[13]sin indeed was in the world before the law was given, but sin is not counted where there is no law. [14]Yet death reigned from Adam to Moses, even over those whose sins were not like the transgression of Adam, who was a type of the one who was to come.

[15]But the free gift is not like the trespass. For if many died through one man's trespass, much more have the grace of God and the free gift in the grace of that one man Jesus Christ abounded for many. [16]And the free gift is not like the effect of that one man's sin. For the judgment following one trespass brought condemnation, but the free gift following many trespasses brings justification. [17]If, because of one man's trespass, death reigned through that one man, much more will those who receive the abundance of grace and the free gift of righteousness reign in life through the one man Jesus Christ.

[18]Then as one man's trespass led to condemnation for all men, so one man's act of righteousness leads to acquittal and life for all men. [19]For as by one man's disobedience many were made sinners, so by one man's obedience many will be made righteous. [20]Law came in, to increase the trespass; but where sin increased, grace abounded all the more, [21]so that, as sin reigned in death, grace also might reign through righteousness to eternal life through Jesus Christ our Lord.

Hitherto we have been shown how Jesus Christ creates a new basis for life. From the life under the Law, which is a life in sin

and under God's wrath, a completely new factor has emerged
by his entry into our world: the life in grace, in the righteousness
of God and in peace with God. Out of evil salvation has come
to all who believe in him. Now the apostle's thought is ready
for the final great effort. In Jesus Christ the stream of mankind's
history as a whole has been guided into a new channel. Previously and apart from him, the stream of the generations rolls
ceaselessly towards a terrible end of destruction—the great
pictures of the judgment of the world with their flow of
human bodies being drawn into the abyss appear before our
view. Jesus Christ orders a halt to this stream of death. He
alters its course; the stream of death becomes a stream of life;
everything that flows into its current is being carried towards
the glorious goal of eternal life.

The stream of death has its origin in the fall of the first man.
His fall is the fall of all, his death the death of all. Mankind is
a unity, and over humanity rules the inexorable law of God that
death is part of sin. It was so from the very beginning. So it was
according to the story on the first pages of the Bible. In the
second chapter of the book "In the beginning" (i.e. Genesis)
the first man was told by God: You will die if you eat of the
forbidden fruit. He did not obey the command, he wantonly
laid hands on what God has reserved for himself. The fall was
followed by the curse and the curse in turn by corruption. Now
death is in the world. When speaking of death Paul does not
merely think of the physical act of dying as a natural event,
so to speak, but of corruption as a power to which human life
has been forfeited, and in connection with the wrath of God
and his terrible judgment. Death is God's destroying power of
wrath and the destined punishment for sin. This power of
death has now entered the world like a murderous plague
seizing every individual human being.

Adam's descendants are not blamelessly seized by this
destructive power, but all perish "because they have sinned".
Paul is not concerned with giving an instructive presentation
of original sin in the sense of the later teaching of the Church.
The physical moment of hereditary transmission is just not
stressed by Paul—that element which since Augustine has
penetrated into the teaching of the Church from ways of
thought alien to the Bible and governed it. There are two

things which concern the apostle. First, since Adam a doom of "death" lies over mankind, over the whole of history; a hostile destructive power has penetrated it, a current that carries off every individual man, leading him towards ruin. No man possesses the strength of himself to flee from this necessity of sinning; everyone shares in this compulsion. Augustine rightly saw in it the meaning of this passage as well as the position of men: They are unable not to sin.

But the second thing is this: that Paul does not call this doom, as such, sin; nor does he even mention a hereditary transmission of sin, but he says that this doom becomes sin by man actually on his own decision acting against God's will and thus becoming a transgressor of the law. It is not the dark, fatal power as such that the apostle calls sin, but one's own self-responsible decision against God's command. He does not want to explain sin by using the well-known phenomenon of the hereditary trans-mission of bad characteristics through natural descent as a means of explanation; this way of directing attention to the process of procreation and natural reproduction is alien to him as it is to biblical thought as a whole. What he wishes to show is the unity of the human race in sin and the subjection of every individual to this terrible compulsion which he receives into his will. Seen from Adam, outside Christ, in its natural historical context, mankind is one in sinning and in subjugation to the power of corruption. As to how this is to be thought of more precisely, Paul says nothing.

Certainly, the special guilt, the fatal leading rôle of the historical ancestor of the race, has been suggested to him and expressly acknowledged by him through the biblical story whose historicity he does not, of course, doubt. It says indeed "because they all have sinned"; but it also says they did not sin in the same manner (not "according to the image of Adam's trespass"). This does not mean that they had already been infected by the necessity to sin, but that unlike Adam they did not sin against an explicitly given command. In the same way it also says, that because of Adam all were included in the condemnation, but not that the later generations were punished for Adam's sin; for it is clearly stated: "Because all men sinned". The main evidence for the Augustinian teaching, in verse 12, "in whom (Adam) all have sinned" was based upon

an obviously false translation of the original Greek text. Later
representatives of the Church's teaching, for instance Calvin,
have, of course, acknowledged and made good this error of
translation, but they permitted themselves to understand
"because they all have sinned" as being applicable since they
had all a sinful nature. If we look through the rest of the letter
to the Romans and the other letters of the apostle we find no
support for the teaching of Augustine. Nowhere does Paul trace
the sin of men back to a hereditary disease. But, of course—
and this is the biblical alternative to the teaching of Pelagius—
he teaches here as everywhere else that since Adam, "death"
in the life of every man is a ruling, insuperable power from
which the individual person, apart from Jesus Christ, seeks in
vain to disentangle himself and which becomes sin in his own
acting and willing. Summing up, we can say this much: Since
Adam this power of sin and death is in the world, and everyone
is implicated in it by being a sinner himself.

But now this section does not intend to speak so much about
Adam and this death-stream as about Jesus Christ and the change
to salvation brought about by him. Paul confronts the picture of mankind's history as it appears since Adam with the
picture of history as represented since Jesus Christ. If mankind
is one in sin and corruption since Adam, that is, as left to itself,
then it is seen in Jesus Christ, the second Adam, also one in
righteousness and life, yes, eternal life. The fact that Paul wants
to express simultaneously two things makes his sentences
particularly difficult to understand. First he wants to say:
There is a correspondence between Adam and Christ; Christ
is the counterpart of Adam; in Christ is being made good what
went wrong through Adam. In Christ the current of history
which had been diverted since Adam from its God-desired
direction towards ruin is once again guided into the right
channel. Christ restores what had been destroyed.

But then Paul is not satisfied with this. Christ is not merely
concerned—this is the second thing—with restoring the
original, of undoing the damage done by Adam, but something
far more. It is at the same time a question of a parallel and a
non-parallel. The gift of grace is greater than the loss; the
saving efficacy of Christ is mightier than the disastrous power
of Adam. Paul is swaying to and fro between the emphasis of

agreement because he feels both things are important enough for him to stress; yet the process of carrying out the one intention prevents the other from ever quite taking a clear form. The total sense, however, is unmistakable. The act of Christ which is here the positive correspondence to Adam's deed weighs more than that deed; world history has been changed through Jesus Christ from a history of disaster into a history of redemption. But this has come about through Christ's act of obedience, which as God's act of reconciliation creates the new position of righteousness by faith whose goal is life eternal.

Here too, however, Paul does not lose sight of the other "position", namely that of law. The Law was not the original thing but has been put in between. That is chiefly meant in a biblical-historical sense: between Adam and Moses lies the time when there was no law. Thus sin, as we have already heard, was at this time different from Adam's sin. This does not mean that Adam therefore stood "under the law"—that does not correspond with the clear statement that the Law has come in between—but that there was for Adam even without the Law a different situation from that of the people between him and Moses, a direct relationship to God as it is at least suggested in the story in Genesis. For Paul here as well as in the letter to the Galatians the Law is no original entity but something provisional, so to speak. For the Law, certain though its divine origin and goodness are, is something that is at the same time annulled in Christ, who fulfils it. Its purpose is indeed God's righteousness; but it cannot provide this. In bestowing this righteousness, Jesus Christ has fulfilled his commission; it is discharged, so to speak. But these are questions which require much more fundamental discussion. The sixth and above all the seventh chapter are devoted to them.

THE NEW LIFE FROM THE DEATH OF CHRIST (6: 1-14)

[1]What shall we say then? Are we to continue in sin that grace may abound? [2]By no means! How can we who died to sin still live in it? [3]Do you not know that all of us who have been baptized into Christ Jesus were baptized into his death? [4]We were buried therefore with him by baptism into death, so that as Christ was raised from the dead by the glory of the Father, we too might walk in newness of life.

⁵For if we have been united with him in a death like his, we shall certainly be united with him in a resurrection like his. ⁶We know that our old self was crucified with him so that the sinful body might be destroyed, and we might no longer be enslaved to sin. ⁷For he who has died is freed from sin. ⁸But if we have died with Christ, we believe that we shall also live with him. ⁹For we know that Christ being raised from the dead will never die again; death no longer has dominion over him. ¹⁰The death he died he died to sin, once for all, but the life he lives he lives to God. ¹¹So you must also consider yourselves dead to sin and alive to God in Christ Jesus.

¹²Let not sin therefore reign in your mortal bodies, to make you obey their passions. ¹³Do not yield your members to sin as instruments of wickedness, but yield yourselves to God as men who have been brought from death to life, and your members to God as instruments of righteousness. ¹⁴For sin will have no dominion over you, since you are not under law but under grace.

Through Jesus Christ man has been placed on a different ground, he has a new position, a position in Christ and therefore in the righteousness of God. This new position has been described first as peace with God, based on Jesus' act of reconciliation. We have been set right with God through the reconciler. God has again received us into his fellowship and we thereby share in that which we lacked previously, in the glory of the divine life. This has come about simply through the divine sovereign acquittal, in the same way as a slave is set free by the stroke of his master's pen. The question immediately is raised: What are we then to do with this freedom? If God puts away our sin in this way, so that the glory of his grace is made to shine, why not aid this shining of his grace a little more by continuing to give God as much opportunity for forgiveness as possible? If an end has been made to morality and grace alone is effectual, why not go ahead then with sinning? If, after all, it does not depend on our own actions, what does it matter how we live? "For everything we do is in vain, even in the best life"—therefore . . . !

Seldom do those who proclaim grace draw this blasphemous conclusion themselves; but their opponents do, who wish to demonstrate from this conclusion the moral danger of the doctrine of grace. Whoever has really understood the meaning of the grace of God cannot even entertain such a thought. Of course, we must add to this: Whether one has really understood the biblical meaning of grace must show itself in one's not drawing such consequences at all. The defence against this terrible misunderstanding provides the apostle with the opportunity to set our relation to Christ in quite a new light. Hitherto it ran: He has suffered for us, he has died for us, he has given us peace. But now it declares that what God says is always a creative word, that the righteousness which he grants us not only produces a new ground, but on this ground also a "new creature" (2 Cor. 5: 17). The Christ who has intervened on our behalf does not remain remote from us, and his righteousness is not merely one belonging to the world beyond. To share in the grace of Christ means to partake of his life; yes, to partake of himself. But where Christ is, there sin must retreat. To live with Christ means: Death to sin!

In order to explain this, Paul touches on the act of baptism. In baptism we have not been submerged in vain. This act of submerging meant death—death to the old man. We have been received into the sphere of Christ by no other way save through his death. This our death, however, like the whole baptism, happened as an act of unification. We have been baptized into the death of Jesus. That means: We enter into his death in faith not only as a death on our behalf, but as our death. He has not only died for us but he died in our place, his death was really valid for us and this sentence of God executed upon him for our salvation we allow to be executed on us. We surrender ourselves into his death, we are crucified with him, we sacrifice our old hitherto sinful life to this death, letting the old man be buried with Christ.

Is this a metaphor, a symbolic action? Certainly, this baptism is a symbolic action, but in it something very real happens. By this surrender to the death of Christ we accept God's judgment on sin as a judgment on us, and in doing so we are separated from sin. Not only is the burden of guilt taken away from us by God's acquittal, but the sinful will is also disposed of. As one finally says farewell at the grave of a person who now lies there below, so by surrendering ourselves into the death of Christ we take leave of the old man. He is

buried now, we have separated ourselves from him with the
same irrevocableness with which Christ has actually died and
been really buried. God's No to sin that he has uttered in the
Cross has now also become our No.

The significance of this No, however, and its force, is the Yes
of God. It is not the death of Jesus but his resurrection which is
God's last word; thus it is not our dying but our life which is
God's purpose. Sin dies with the life of Christ; it loses its power
because Christ's power gains control over us. Our No to sin is
not primary but is the answer to God's Yes to us. Since God is
claiming us for himself, sin has no longer any claim on us. We
belong to God now; in separating us from sin he binds us to
himself. The death which Christ died is the breaking through
of God's life. Sin is nothing in itself and its destruction is not
an end in itself. Sin is that which obstructs God, therefore it
must disappear. It is removed so that God may receive what
belongs to him. Already here we catch a glimpse of the next
theme: Death and sin belong together. Because Christ by his
death has given death its due, so to speak, this death has no
longer any claim on him. The resurrection is the meaning of
the death on the Cross. After the enemy of life, sin, has been
overpowered, there is thus no longer anything left for Death.
Life, however, the real life liberated from its adversary, is the
life from God and for God. This life knows no more death. It is
life eternal.

Thus we too who are baptized, in having not only been
submerged but also having emerged again, have been im-
mersed not only into the death of Christ, but above all into his
life, his resurrected life, his divine life. This has a twofold
meaning. First—and this is only touched upon here—we shall
one day share in the resurrection of Jesus Christ; we too, thanks
to our having been ingrafted into his life, shall march through
death into his life, as he through death has entered into eternal
life. Baptism makes us partakers of the future resurrection.

Secondly—and it is this which stands now in the foreground
—we share already, now, in the new life. We are dead now unto
sin and alive for God. But then the provisional aspect of our
present position of life, our position of faith, shows itself in
that this new life does not merely exist but claims us too, and
must be realized through our willing. Thus it does not run:

You are walking now in a new life. Where the rebirth is spoken of in this way, there the line of a sober sense of reality is being relinquished. Rather: You ought also to walk in the new life now! Baptism is therefore not a magical event, efficacious with the irresistibility of something in the course of nature, but it is a spiritual event which always continues to be "ethically" mediated, and must therefore always be affirmed by us.

The Christian who has truly said Yes to Christ and truly No to sin, who knows himself to be united with Christ through God's acquittal, through justification and baptism, is now not only simply rid of sin in the sense that it has altogether disappeared from his field of vision; but he has no longer anything to do with it, he pays no more attention to it, he knows that he belongs now to God. We still, of course, live in a mortal body; dying as yet does not lie behind us, though it certainly has been deprived of its terror, its essential meaning. Therefore sin is also still in front of our door, so to speak, desiring to be let in again. Now is the time to defend the new position of life against it. It has no longer any business with us. We are no longer of any importance to it whatsoever; we are "dead to sin" as sin is dead to us.

There is here also an ought: sin ought not to reign. But this ought is now no longer that of "the categorical imperative", the Law; it rather emerges out of a new reality. Man is through Christ someone who has risen from death to life. The foreigner in our life is not the ought, as was the case before, but sin. Previously, the ought did not suit us, now sin does not. For previously we were "in sin"; now we are "in Christ". Previously the law came from outside, so to speak, into our "own" and otherwise disposed life. Now the new life for God is our proper life and sin wants to invade it. This "outside" is, of course, quite close to us: our own mortal body is, as it were, the hiding-place of sin, from which it continues to attack us. Not that the body as such was the origin of sin—this is the Greek way of thinking, not the biblical—but the body is, so to speak, still unconquered territory from which sin, once it has penetrated into it, is hard to dislodge.

The reminder, therefore, of sin dwelling in the body does not stand in opposition to the central biblical and also Pauline teaching that the origin of sin is to be found in the spirit.

51

Quite the contrary. As sin has its origin at the centre of the
person, in his relation to God, so the re-conquest of man from
God's side, in Christ, also takes place from this centre. First
this centre is set right; man through the justification of the
sinner and by faith is first led back to full dependence on God,
and then the conquest advances from the centre to the peri-
phery, right into the bodily nature. The honour belongs to
God alone, we have and receive everything solely from God;
once the centre of the person has been led back into the truth,
then the other thing can also be set in order. But to begin with,
sin is still there and continues to be present, in the unredeemed
realm from which, so to speak, it makes its sorties in order to
regain what had been snatched away. Under the Law it was
exactly the reverse; there was indeed a far-reaching possibility
of self-education, yet the effort never came near the innermost
being, just because it was the effort of the "I" myself. But now
God Himself "apart from the law" has newly created the
innermost being, the relation to himself. Here there is no
longer any ought, but only the gift which was appropriated in
faith; this new status, however, must now be defended and
spread abroad, so to speak. This is the new ought.

The meaning of this ought is clear: It concerns living-for-
God. It is the meaning of the new life as it is the meaning of
the life of Christ. It is from the very beginning life-for-God.
As such it is laid hold of in faith. I belong to God. But what
matters now is to "carry across" this living-for-God into
physical reality. The members of the body must now quite
actually become the instruments of God. The metaphor of
conquest is not strange to Paul; he speaks of "weapons and
righteousness for God", that is of the holy war. For it concerns
the question of reigning, the extension of God's rule throughout
the entire practical sphere of life, the re-conquest of what
originally belonged to God but had rebelliously turned apostate.
All this must now become subject to God again, not as if he
were an alien power but as the rightful Lord who is acknowledged as such. Accordingly faith has understood it thus: I now
belong to God; this must also become true in my daily life.
What does this amount to, then?

52

THE VICTORY OVER SIN (6: 15-23)

¹⁵What then? Are we to sin because we are not under law but under grace? By no means! ¹⁶Do you not know that if you yield yourselves to any one as obedient slaves, you are slaves of the one whom you obey, either of sin, which leads to death, or of obedience, which leads to righteousness? ¹⁷But thanks be to God, that you who were once slaves of sin have become obedient from the heart to the standard of teaching to which you were committed, ¹⁸and, having been set free from sin, have become slaves of righteousness. ¹⁹I am speaking in human terms, because of your natural limitations. For just as you once yielded your members to impurity and to greater and greater iniquity, so now yield your members to righteousness for sanctification.

²⁰When you were slaves of sin, you were free in regard to righteousness. ²¹But then what return did you get from the things of which you are now ashamed? The end of those things is death. ²²But now that you have been set free from sin and have become slaves of God, the return you get is sanctification and its end, eternal life. ²³For the wages of sin is death, but the free gift of God is eternal life in Christ Jesus our Lord.

Since we men are what we are, the word *grace*, the great word of the faith, is continually interpreted in a sinful misunderstanding. As soon as it says, Free from the Law, the sinful flesh scents the morning breeze. And on the other side, legal Pharisaism gets ready to draw dangerous conclusions from the doctrine of grace in order to destroy it. These two hostile brothers, lawlessness and legalism, are indeed with us and in us all the time. The one sees in grace its opportunity, the other its enemy. Thus faith in Christ has continually to fight on two fronts. Both sides declare: Freedom from the Law and therefore a free course for sin! It goes without saying that there can be no question of this here. How could you . . . do you not know? But the time has now come for showing why this is an impossible misunderstanding.

Freedom from the Law does not mean freedom from God but freedom for God. For faith is the exact opposite from being loosed from God; it is not an indirect but an immediate relationship with God. Faith knows: I belong to God from the very start. Whereas the law of "ought" asks me, as it were, whether I wish to belong to and obey God, faith does not allow this question to be raised at all. There is no need to ask any questions; this is so "from the very beginning". Therefore faith belongs to obedience as a matter of course.

Yet Paul is not satisfied with establishing this. For the question at stake is not really obedience or non-obedience. Man is made in such a way that he must always be obedient; the question only is: obedient to whom? "Freedom in general" is an illusion, something impossible. The only choice before man is whom he wants to obey; never whether he wishes to be obedient. Either he obeys God, or he obeys sin. Is this not just a fancy? Is there not an entity which I myself am, palmed off by me as an "other", personified sin? What is the meaning of being obedient to sin? Paul certainly knows that he is "speaking in human terms". Nevertheless things are really as he states them.

Man in sin is the "slave of sin". Sin itself is absence of freedom. Man is no longer master of himself, for when he sins he becomes entangled in sin and thus a prisoner. Man can indeed step on to this inclined plane; once he is on it he glides down, whether he wants to or not. John found the right expression for it: Everyone who commits sin is a slave to sin (8: 34). Man cannot step out of the path of existence shown to him by God; he can only march on it forward or backward. Going backward is sin, going forward is faith. There is only this either—or; no open plain beside it.

This, however, means that the man who sins is destroying himself. When man goes back along this path, it leads him to numbness and dissolution and then death. The fruit of sin, looked at in the light and seen in its individual parts, is never delightful but "things of which you must be ashamed". And the net result is death. Sin is destruction, above all and first, self-destruction. Human life which contradicts its law of creation disintegrates. For if it be true that man "by right", i.e. on account of creation, belongs to God, then this opposition towards God can only lead to dissolution. No doctrine of freedom can alter this in the slightest. Sliding down the inclined plane may at first look splendid; one can give oneself up to the enjoyment of freedom from God like that prodigal son who made his father pay him the money. But the illusion does not last for ever; the consequences of the dissolution, which at first are only of a quite inward and delicate sort, continue to become more massive and lend themselves less and less to being changed into a lie as something positive. The concealed bankruptcy becomes open, the prodigal son finds himself one day in unmistakable misery among the swine. The inner lawlessness leads to the manifestly lawless, undisciplined existence, the ending in nothing comes into sight, even if it does not reveal itself in its complete nothingness, its final character of death. Thus matters stand with the supposed freedom.

But what about the supposed lack of freedom, that "absence of freedom" because of which the Fall happened and continues to happen, what about obedience to God? It also has its logic, it has a path and a goal, too. It is exactly the counterpart of the first. It is the way of life and its goal is eternal life. How should it be otherwise? After all it is life in God, therefore life within life. To be free from sin is the only real freedom; freedom from sin, however, is obedience towards God. "Slaves of righteousness", most certainly! But what does being a slave mean? Here too it is a question of "must", an inner necessity, but the inner necessity which is in accordance with the purpose of our creation, union with him who in this union gives meaning, support and strength to our life. It is the union which constitutes life, the being together in contrast to the being apart, the way of salvation as opposed to the deadly disintegration. Here it is also true: Whoever treads this path catches sight of the goal, without, however, having already arrived there; but it is the opposite goal from death, eternal life.

With freedom from the Law matters stand like this: If it is that freedom from the Law which is lawlessness, then its end is death. But if it is the freedom which is constraint to God, then its end is life, unconditional, simply life, eternal life. This second path, however, can only be trodden through Jesus Christ. He it is who sets us free from the Law in such a way that he now joins us all the more to God, binding us to him.

FREEDOM FROM THE LAW (7: 1-6)

[1]Do you not know, brethren—for I am speaking to those who know the law—that the law is binding on a person only

during his life? ²Thus a married woman is bound by law to her husband as long as he lives; but if her husband dies she is discharged from the law concerning the husband. ³Accordingly, she will be called an adulteress if she lives with another man while her husband is alive. But if her husband dies she is free from that law, and if she marries another man she is not an adulteress.

⁴Likewise, my brethren, you have died to the law through the body of Christ, so that you may belong to another, to him who has been raised from the dead in order that we may bear fruit for God. ⁵While we were living in the flesh, our sinful passions, aroused by the law, were at work in our members to bear fruit for death. ⁶But now we are discharged from the law, dead to that which held us captive, so that we serve not under the old written code but in the new life of the Spirit.

But what is the position now in regard to the Law? Hitherto it has only been shown that through Christ there exists a new basis for life, a new ground "apart from the law", and that an entirely new life grows out of this soil. It has also already been shown, at least in a preliminary fashion, that what the Law demanded in it is making itself felt all the more. But the statement that Christians are free from the Law has hitherto been asserted rather than proved. And yet it is an assertion of tremendous significance. Paul is not dealing with pagans for whom this question would be of no consequence or unintelligible, but with a community at whose worship the Old Testament was regularly read as the Word of God. To take the responsibility of saying that Christians are free from the Law— from God's Law!—this is certainly no light or safe matter. The entire seventh chapter and part of the eighth is a wrestling on the part of the apostle, continually starting anew, with this difficult and ever decisive problem of faith in Christ.

First Paul tries to make his thesis understood and to prove it by way of a simile. He chooses an example from marriage law to make it clear that the Law has no validity, no binding power beyond death. This simile, however, is very far from constituting a proof; in several ways it is extremely vulnerable. For to start with, other and just as good legal maxims could be found, for instance, in the Old Testament, which assert the opposite, its binding power beyond death. Secondly, the simile is faulty

in that there first of all one person is set free by the death of the
other, here, however, by his own death; and then, also, in so
far as there the dying person and the survivor are always
different persons, here they are the same. Yet precisely through
this fault in the simile it becomes clear that what Paul means
concerns something entirely unique and outside all natural
comparisons. Yes, in reality, the dying and the surviving
person is one and the same: the man who by baptism into the
death of Christ dies himself and who through this dying comes
to life again. Yet the question of binding and loosing also cannot be grasped through any human comparisons. For previously
man was not bound to someone but something, to the impersonal entity called "law"; but now to someone, namely the
living Christ.

And thus not only the point of reference of the binding but
the mode of binding has entirely changed. Being tied to the
Law was something of quite a different kind from being bound
to Christ. This shows itself especially in the effect of these two
different kinds of binding. Man bound to the Law produced
the "fruit of death", man bound to Christ the "fruit of life".

A new problem is raised alongside this, which will be
specially clarified in the following section. There exists a
strange connection between sin and law. It is not as if the Law
were to be made responsible for sin—this conclusion Paul de-
cisively rejects in the next section; but where sin once is, there
the Law can be effective only in the sense that it evokes and
intensifies this sin more than ever. It causes the sin lying within
us to break out and to mature. This fruit of sin, moreover, as
we were taught in the previous chapter, is the fruit of death.
It is therefore, so to speak, a twofold death which we die in the
baptism of Christ: a dying to sin and a dying to the law. These
three entities belong together in a mysterious way; they are, as
it were, one and the same firm: Sin, Law, and Death. Thus to
be set free from one is also simultaneously a deliverance from
the others; equally the liberation from one can only take place
if the deliverance from the two others also happens. Without
the liberation from the Law there is no deliverance from sin
and death.

This liberation is now, however, no mere beautiful thought
but an experienced reality. We are set free from the Law, we

are dead, to sin as well as the Law. And the product of life has thus become an entirely different one: we now bear fruit no longer to death, but to God. Hence a final contrast becomes manifest. We have already said that the mode of binding has become a completely new one through the change of the point of reference of the binding. This newness Paul denotes by the antitheses: Imprisonment within the Law or the old existence of the letter on the one side, freedom or the new existence of the Spirit on the other. Being bound to the Law is captivity, being bound to the living Christ is freedom. There it is enslavement to the letter, here freedom in the Holy Spirit; a theme which the apostle will mightily develop in the eighth chapter.

THE LAW AS AN INSTRUMENT OF SIN (7: 7-13)

[7]What then shall we say? That the law is sin? By no means! Yet, if it had not been for the law, I should not have known sin. I should not have known what it is to covet if the law had not said, "You shall not covet". [8]But sin, finding opportunity in the commandment, wrought in me all kinds of covetousness. Apart from the law sin lies dead. [9]I was once alive apart from the law, but when the commandment came, sin revived and I died; [10]the very commandment which promised life proved to be death to me. [11]For sin, finding opportunity in the commandment, deceived me and by it killed me. [12]So the law is holy, and the commandment is holy and just and good.

[13]Did that which is good, then, bring death to me? By no means! It was sin, working death in me through what is good, in order that sin might be shown to be sin, and through the commandment might become sinful beyond measure.

If this is the position with the three entities of sin, law and death, as we have just stated, then the question forces itself upon us: Is then the Law itself a power opposed to God, is it itself sin? There can be no question of this. The Law is indeed God's Law, his will and therefore holy, just and good. Thus it is not the fault of the Law if it leads to death. It is no ally of sin. And yet it operates as if it were so; quite against its meaning, it has a working relationship with sin. Once man is in the grip of the power of sin, then the Law not only proves itself ineffective as a power opposing it, which it really ought to be, but even contributes as a decisive factor towards the maturing of sin. It makes me even more familiar with sin. This is not only to be understood in the sense that the Law is the rule of what is good, with which we measure, and therefore recognize, evil as evil. The intertwining of law and sin is much closer and more of a unity. The Law enters into the process of the formation of sin, it is itself a factor in becoming sinful. This is illustrated by a generally well-known fact: the commandment, or rather the prohibition, irritates one directly into sinning. It is like a sun that rouses the still dormant seed of sin, causing it to sprout. It makes sin alive, drawing it forth and strengthening it continually.

But the apostle does not merely remind us of something that has long been known and keeps on happening. He is not concerned with a psychology of sin, though he certainly begins with a psychological observation; his glance penetrates deeper into the secret of the origin of sin. From what is merely psychological, that is, from what everyone continually experiences and perceives, he passes over to the historical aspect, showing us, in speaking of his personal history, the history of sin in mankind; he thus takes up the line of thought of chapter 5: 12ff. but gives this a new turn by referring to his own history.

I was once alive without the Law. What is meant by this "once"? Childhood? Is Paul telling us of the various periods of his life? Apart from the fact that this would be very strange in the case of Paul, it can hardly be materially harmonized with his explanations. Paul rather shows, in saying "I", how matters stand with man and humanity in general; he is not relating a story, but is interpreting through faith the history of mankind as the history of each individual. The passage is thus to be understood neither psychologically nor biographically nor world-historically, but theologically. What has been said in connection with Genesis 3 in the fifth chapter (page 44ff.) concerning the fall of Adam is presupposed. Sin is in the world, it does not just arise. But the individual person is as yet not a sinner. Sin is dead for him at first, thus he on the contrary is alive. Now comes the Law and along with it sin. It revives with the arrival of the Law. How is that to be understood? Does it mean: Previously there was lust but I did not know

59

that lust is evil, therefore sin was as yet not present? Surely not. The rôle of the Law is a more active one. Only in face of the Law does man, in so far as he is just not in fellowship with God, come into the position of making a decision.

Whether child or simple minded, he is not a transgressor, apart from God's demand. Sin is a spiritual act in regard to God's demand. The Law is the only thing, apart from the grace of Christ, about which man can come to a decision. And now the decision is made in the negative sense. This is the primal fact behind which we cannot go. It is simply a fact; going back to Adam's fall does not help at all. Just as it previously ran that death came on all from Adam because all have sinned, so it runs now: At the Law, I became a sinner, and with me every-body else. In this respect sin is in the world, thus it is present as a power, thus it makes its appearance. Paul therefore does not say with the Church's doctrine of original sin that man is already a sinner from the very beginning, tainted with Adam's curse: nor does he say with the idealistic moralists that man could, if he wished, also decide otherwise, namely against sin. He simply observes that this is the case with all and that sin is just the power under which man stands as soon as the decision has to be made.

The fact that the Law, which is divine, holy and good, has this effect, is without doubt not the fault of the Law but of sin. And yet we ought to remind ourselves here of the earlier thought that the Law has come in between. Perhaps both are one and the same fact seen from two sides, namely, that sin is present and that God's holy will becomes understandable to us and known to us only in the form of the Law. To this points the fact that Paul never simply says (though it might have been near to his heart as a true son of Israel) that the Law came because God gave it. We have to conclude from other state-ments (Gal. 3 and 4; Rom. 5 and 10) that it is no accident that Paul, for whom the Law in spite of its divine character is some-thing unoriginal and alien, wanted to say with the neutral "the Law came" something other than that which the pious Jew and commonly also the pious Christian reads out of the history of the Mosaic legislation. The Law, although in its essence from God, is nevertheless in its legal, purely commanding form, linked with sin from the beginning. The Mosaic legislation is for him divided into two basically different component parts: The promise of grace pointing to Jesus Christ which claims man (Rom. 4; Gal. 4) and the naked Law which as such belongs with sin although it is the representative of God's holy will.

From this it becomes clear that the Law is considered here only in its negative, sin-awakening and sin-increasing effect. If the Law stands over against man, if the Law is on the level on which he stands, then it cannot be otherwise. The Law produces wrath, brings sin to life; the letter of the Law kills in contrast to the life-giving Spirit (2 Cor. 3: 6). But, let it be repeated, that is not the fault of the Law itself, but of its connection with sin. And in this way, too, the Law fulfils a divine mission: it makes sin manifest, it makes it break out, it brings it to terrible maturity and thus makes the cure possible. For it creates the knowledge of sin; without the knowledge of sin there is also no justifying faith. In that the Law is able to do just this in its deadly effect, it shows once again that in origin it is God's law and therefore holy, just and good.

THE POWERLESSNESS OF THE LAW (7: 14-25)

[14]We know that the law is spiritual; but I am carnal, sold under sin. [15]I do not understand my own actions. For I do not do what I want, but I do the very thing I hate. [16]Now if I do what I do not want, I agree that the law is good. [17]So then it is no longer I that do it, but sin which dwells within me. [18]For I know that nothing good dwells within me, that is, in my flesh. I can will what is right, but I cannot do it. [19]For I do not do the good I want, but the evil I do not want is what I do. [20]Now if I do what I do not want, it is no longer I that do it, but sin which dwells within me.

[21]So I find it to be a law that when I want to do right, evil lies close at hand. [22]For I delight in the law of God, in my inmost self, [23]but I see in my members another law at war with the law of my mind and making me captive to the law of sin which dwells in my members. [24]Wretched man that I am! Who will deliver me from this body of death? [25]Thanks be to God through Jesus Christ our Lord! So then, I of myself serve the law of God with my mind, but with my flesh I serve the law of sin.

It is an old controversy, and indeed one on which not only

theologians but also Churches have parted company and still diverge: Of whom is Paul speaking here? Who is this unhappy man crying out for deliverance? Is it the Christian Paul, the re-born man, as is, of course, suggested at first by the present tense of all the statements? Or is it Paul before his conversion, that Saul who knew indeed the law of God but persecuted Christ; of whom the entire context of the chapter speaks, dealing as it does with man under the Law? Can a man who does not know Christ speak in this way about sin, feel the opposition between sin and the will of God in this manner, and can he speak thus of the inward man and his approval of the Law as the "I" of verses 14-25 does? say the advocates of the first view. Can a Christian or an apostle, indeed can the Paul who in chapter 6 of Romans has described the new life of the Christian as a renunciation of sin, speak in this way of himself, as a wretched man sold to sin? say the others. Obviously the problem is a little too complicated to be solved by a single Yes or No.

There can be no question at all but that Paul speaks here also of the man under the Law, as he did in the first half of the chapter. The train of thought continues without a break. The Law does not save me against and from sin but fills to the brim the measure of sin. Nevertheless it is of a spiritual kind. Hence, the Law in its spiritual nature, in contrast to and yet at the same time with a peculiar reciprocal effect upon sin, is mainly the theme here, too. But now the problem is complicated by the fact that, exactly corresponding to that which we said above on the duality of the Law, man is now being considered from a double point of view; namely, inasmuch as he is turned to the Law and also to sin.

Even man outside Christ knows the Law, of course, be he Jew or Gentile; and in recognizing it as the Law, as the valid norm, he somehow also affirms it. There is—here the idealism of all times is right and the historical reality speaks for it quite unambiguously—in every relatively normal person a knowledge of a categorical imperative, and with this knowledge also a rational acknowledgment of its validity (else it were simply not a categorical imperative). And because this is so, there exists also a contradiction in man, which everyone experiences in the fact of his bad conscience. Is it this, therefore, of which Paul is speaking? Does he speak of that experience which Ovid has expressed in his famous "video meliora proboque, deteriora sequor" (I perceive the better and approve of it but I follow that which is worse)? Yes and no. Of course, Paul speaks of this contradiction in man, of him who is under the Law, who does not know Christ. Only he who disrupts the order of the verses can deny this. And yet, the Christian Paul speaks quite differently from the heathen Ovid of the misery of man under the Law! Paul thus does not speak of what man outside Christ knows of himself but of how matters really stand with the godless man, the man outside Christ; hence of how as a Christian one understands this reality of being outside Christ. This is the one thing upon which the blunt Yes or No is wrecked.

There is, however, another thing. Why does Paul, although keeping to the theme of verses 1-13, pass of a sudden in verse 14 into the present tense? Is this simply a literary fancy? Hardly! The mere necessity of a change would hardly have been able to move a Paul to such a striking alteration of style. He does it rather because he no longer wishes to speak of something simply past as before but of something somehow still present. That is not only conjecture. For here at this point Paul introduces a concept which he has not used before in verses 1-13: The flesh.

The flesh is, of course, something to which a man even in Christ is still bound. In the life of him who is now standing on the new ground there is still also to be found that lair of sin from which it continues to make a raid into his new life. Thus the flesh is that part which materially links the new being with the old. Therefore, in so far as even the Christian not only has the flesh but, abandoning the new position, slips back again into the old and lives "according to the flesh", he lives again in sin and under the Law, thus being the man who is described in the seventh chapter. The second part, too, deals with the Christian, namely in so far as he is not in Christ but in sin; its theme is precisely the same as that of the first part, man under the Law, that is, man outside Christ.

That is the second thing which makes impossible a simple Yes or No to the question put at the beginning. Paul, the Christian, shows what it really means to be outside Christ;

63

and Paul, the Christian, speaks of it as being also a possibility for the Christian position which continually threatens and continually becomes a reality. We have now constructed in detail an approach to the understanding of this.

In man outside Christ there is a contradiction between law and sin, or between the acknowledgment of the Law and the desire of the flesh. But the question here no longer pertains to the desire of the flesh but to a second law, the "law in my members" whose substance or effect is that, in spite of willing the good, evil emerges, and which is therefore directly called a law of sin. Alongside the law of God there is thus put an antithesis and the struggle now is no longer between sinful desire and the Law but between two laws; that is, between two kinds of necessity. Over against the ideal necessity—thou shalt do good, I actually intended to do good, indeed—stands the real necessity—I am sold to sin, I must sin.

That Paul has really in view the man under the Law follows also from the fact that he defines God's law as "the law of my mind." It is not the cause, as Greek philosophy maintained, but the consequence of sin that man is thus divided. On the one side an irrational flesh, on the other an ineffectual law of reason! On the one side fleshly desire, on the other a powerless approval of the law of God! How could it be otherwise! Paul does not know anything of man in the abstract, he only knows of man as God's creation, created in the image of God. This man cannot, if he turns away from God, if he is in sin, live in any other way than in contradiction not only towards God but also towards himself. He cannot transform himself; he can only pervert God's creation, bring it out of order, that is, out of its unity, into contradiction. The most profound contradiction, or the contradiction in its depth, is that of the will and the action running in opposite directions.

So, does Paul not deny to man under the Law his good will but only the doing of the good? We must be on our guard here not to quarrel about words. When Luther or Calvin deny a good will to man under the Law, they understand by it something entirely different from what is meant here by approval of the Law and delight in the Law. They simply mean a will that leads to action, since the same action, of course, if it is already good, cannot be anything but the product of the

64

truly good will. This good will, Paul is indeed denying to man; he only uses different words. He says: We will the good, indeed, but we do not do it. Why does he speak at all of a willing of the good, even of a delight in the good? One might say, first of all, that he knows this simply as a fact from his Pharisaic past. Yet he is not merely dealing with the Pharisee but with man in general in so far as he stands under the Law. Even to him he does not deny such a "will" and "delight". Why not? Simply because it is a fact. The Gentile as well as the atheist knows something of this delight in the good, this approval of the Law, even though he swears a thousand times that he does not believe in God. We are not here concerned with the atheist; but one thing is clear: Just as Paul does not entirely deny to the Gentile the knowledge of the Law, so he also does not deny him a certain delight in the Law, a certain approval of it; in which case the Gentile, of course, does not know whose law it is. Paul the Christian knows that, the Jew Saul possibly knows it.

It is strange that Paul compares the mind that delights in the Law and serves it as the inward man, with the members. Here it becomes very clear that he thinks not only of a past existence under the Law but of one which continually becomes a grievous experience for the Christian. Else he would scarcely have used the expression "inward man". But that in fact he simply means the man outside Christ is clearly shown by his final sentence: "Serving the law of God with my mind, but with my flesh I serve the law of sin."

If one asks further: Surely sin does not reside in the mind but only in the lust of the flesh? the answer must be in the negative. On the contrary, the fact that the mind is so powerless, the will so lame and unreal—this is the power of sin in the mind. What else could it be but sin which deprives the willing of the good of so much strength that it cannot lead to action? The "sinful" flesh is of course not called this because it is the cause of sin, but because it has been infected by sin. For sin has its real seat in the heart of man (Rom. 1: 21, 24). In our context nothing is said explicitly here of the darkening of the mind; elsewhere, however, it is mentioned by Paul (e.g. Eph. 4: 18).

One could head this section "Concerning the misery of man". The contradiction in human nature, the contrast between his will and action, must be a misery. It is impossible not to be a "wretched man" if one does that which one hates and does not do that in which one takes delight. How could one be anything but wretched if one is being torn apart by two opposed necessities? There may be a kind of suffering which, like bodily pain for instance, is more violent, more stunning in its effect; but there is no suffering which goes deeper than that of the inner cleavage. Here too it is the hand of Paul the Christian that improves on the quite obscure lines which the non-Christian draws when speaking of this misery, improving and above all bringing into relief what is essential, focussing everything on what is essential. But, whether he feels it more deeply or less, this misery, truly considered, is the condition of man outside Christ and that of the Christian always in so far as he places himself outside Christ, in so far as he lapses.

This section, therefore, cannot end on any other note but that of a cry for help. Yet even with this cry for help the apostle's thought proceeds still further. The theme of "death" is taken up once more after it had for a time disappeared from view. In death, every kind of misery, all dissolution agglomerates. The cleavage within man is a mortal wound, something that must lead to death; and we must remember that death here always means something total, not merely physical death, and not merely an extinction, but a negative existence. The solid bearer and expression of this corruption of death is the body, the same body in whose members the law of sin finds its support, so to speak. This is why it is called a body of death.

The cry for help does not fade away. The answer is already here. Not an answer that is heard for the first time but one already known: God be thanked for Jesus Christ. He is the answer, the deliverance. This is the subject which is now to be treated.

FREEDOM AND LIFE IN THE SPIRIT (8: 1-17)

[1]There is therefore now no condemnation for those who are in Christ Jesus. [2]For the law of the Spirit of life in Christ Jesus has set me free from the law of sin and death. [3]For God has done what the law, weakened by the flesh, could not do: sending his own Son in the likeness of sinful flesh and for sin, he condemned sin in the flesh, [4]in order that the just requirement of the law might be fulfilled in us, who walk not according to the flesh

but according to the Spirit. ⁵For those who live according to the flesh set their minds on the things of the flesh, but those who live according to the Spirit set their minds on the things of the Spirit. ⁶To set the mind on the flesh is death, but to set the mind on the Spirit is life and peace. ⁷For the mind that is set on the flesh is hostile to God; it does not submit to God's law, indeed it cannot; ⁸and those who are in the flesh cannot please God.

⁹But you are not in the flesh, you are in the Spirit, if the Spirit of God really dwells in you. Any one who does not have the Spirit of Christ does not belong to him. ¹⁰But if Christ is in you, although your bodies are dead because of sin, your spirits are alive because of righteousness. ¹¹If the Spirit of him who raised Jesus from the dead dwells in you, he who raised Christ Jesus from the dead will give life to your mortal bodies also through his Spirit which dwells in you.

Another page is turned. The theme, however, is none other than that developed from the fifth chapter, with the interruption, of course, of chapter seven: The new life, the life from or in the righteousness of God, by faith in the reconciliation through Jesus Christ. With a sharp turn Paul breaks off the reflections on man under the Law, again a "now" stands here as the signal of the new train of thought or rather the old one taken up once more. We now, of course, stand no longer on the deadly ground of the Law but on the ground of life newly created through Christ. But from here we glance back to the one just left, and compare these two opposite ways of life.

The decisive point is quite briefly put at the beginning: No longer condemnation. The Law is now described in the very sharpest comprehensive terms: Law of sin and death. We have been set free from it. Yet here, too, after having already briefly glanced provisionally, as it were, at the glories of the new life—the being in Christ, Spirit, Life, Freedom—we are once more referred, by way of a most powerful recapitulation, to the event upon which the new position of life is founded: the act of reconciliation through Christ. Here a condemnation has taken place. Thus without such a condemnation there is no new life. That is the meaning of God sending his Son, his coming in the form of sinful flesh. In him sin was to be judged and simultaneously the demand of the righteousness of the Law fulfilled, which the Law, owing to our sinful weakness, was

unable to effect in us. God's demand of righteousness is not
in some way cancelled but fulfilled. Yet not through us but
through himself.

And God's judgment on sin is not pushed aside but carried
out, yet not on us but on him, the Son in whom God acts. That
is the secret of this man and this event. In him God acts—
reconciling and revealing; and in him mankind experiences—
through atonement—the punishment for its sinful, fleshly
nature; and in this his suffering of punishment the demand of
righteousness is satisfied; that which the Law demands is
fulfilled. Paul here sums up in one single sentence what he had
stated in greater detail in the third chapter. And yet he is not
merely saying the same thing. The theme there is now en-
larged by the knowledge of the subsequent chapters: the
powerlessness of the Law, the connection between flesh and
sin, the necessity of sin lying upon humanity. Thus Christ's
reconciling act can be looked at from a new angle. God's Son
had to assume the sinful flesh of humanity in order to be able
to bear and take away its burden. Godhead and manhood had
to be in an incomprehensible manner united in it so that God's
law could be really fulfilled.

But now above all the direction is new in which the effect of
the act of reconciliation is seen in our life. And with this we
come to the main theme of this section: The life of the Spirit.
Previously the question of the Spirit was only touched on in
passing. Only now, after sin and law have been so thoroughly
dealt with, can it be rightly understood how the life in the
Spirit is achieved. It is nothing else than "being in Christ".
Whoever belongs to Christ by faith becomes a vessel of the
Holy Spirit; the Spirit "dwells" in him. Here too Paul speaks
of a "law", a law of the Spirit, a necessity, an order; but this
order had precisely the characteristics which are in opposition
to those of the "law of death": freedom, life, righteousness.
Freedom as direct union with God; life through participation
in God's glory; righteousness by the new creation of the will.

For now what the sixth chapter has already demonstrated
in other words becomes all the clearer: the righteousness of
Christ does not remain alien to us, opposite, in the beyond; it
is not solely imputed to us, but is also "fulfilled in us, who walk
not according to the flesh but according to the Spirit". The

new life is a new righteousness, not merely any longer as the "ground" of justification on which we stand, but also as the strength of a new walking, a new conduct of life. Paul here calls the origin of all human conduct of life a "being minded", the innermost tendency of the will and thought. The new life shows itself in the fact that here also, in this direction of the will, the same contrast of once and now asserts itself as did between law-flesh-death and freedom-spirit-life.

In the old status of life, in "the walking after the flesh", thought and will are directed towards what is "fleshly". A passion for the world and selfishness rule us; the creature, not the Creator, is our point of orientation. We wish to make the things of the world our own and to assert ourselves in the world. The will passes God by, it avoids God, thus showing that in the last resort it is hostile towards God. If I shun anyone, I do not want to have anything to do with him. In withdrawing from God, I eliminate him so far as I am concerned. I am hostile to him. And in doing this, I shape my life in a way to which God cannot say Yes but only No. However much that is good, beautiful and true, however much culture and humanity may realize themselves in this way, there is only a shattering judgment to be expected from God, because the innermost tendency of all this formation is opposed to God.

But now matters are indeed different, since "Christ dwells in us". A new power of life, God's Spirit, has now taken possession of man, giving a new direction to his thought and will. Man now no longer "minds" what is fleshly but the things of the Spirit. Just as little as the flesh meant the sensual or physical, so the things of the Spirit do not mean here what we call, for instance, "spiritual" life: culture, art, science, philosophy and such like. The Spirit that is meant here is not the spirit of man, not the "spiritual", but God's Spirit. One may confidently interpret the thought in this way: You now "mind" things divine or God's Kingdom. Accordingly a new condition sets in, life and peace. Destruction and unrest, the inner conflict, belongs to enmity against God; that which is life-creating, truly edifying, the innermost peace, belongs to friendship towards God.

Thus here, too, the one form of life is quite clearly opposed to the other, as a complete contrast to it. The question only

is: Is that really the case then? Is it not, say, a fine theory, a
mere idea? is it a fact of experience? At first it is only said, quite
simply: You are now in the Spirit. Yet this is not merely
asserted; Paul appeals here to an experienced reality. The
Spirit "dwells indeed in you". By this is not meant some special
occult endowment or some peculiar mystical experience, but
the fundamental fact of the Christian Life. Here the whole
is involved. There are not Christians, those belonging to
Christ, who have the Spirit, and others who do not have the
Spirit. Having the Spirit and having Christ is one and the same
thing; or they are directly connected in such a way that one
cannot separate them or hardly distinguish between them.
Therefore it is put in plain words: If you have not the Spirit
then you are also without Christ. Paul says this here also, as he
does to the Corinthians, for the sake of self-examination: "Test
yourselves whether Christ is in you!" (2 Cor. 13: 5).

Is faith then not enough? Of course faith is enough; by the
word faith Paul again and again paraphrases the whole
Christian position. But what he means by faith is here put in a
new way. True faith is the same thing as "having the Spirit",
the same as "Christ dwells in me". In faith God's Spirit lays
hold on us, and only in so far as God's Spirit enters into us does
true faith really come about. How this is actually meant
emerges from the following:

"Christ in you" not only signifies a new spiritual bent but
at the same time a real participation in his life, in the glory of
his resurrection. To be sure, we are still tied to this earthly,
transitory world through our bodies. Yet this bodily nature has
not only no longer any claim upon us but also no power where
Christ reigns. "He who believes in me, though he die yet has he
eternal life", is the way John puts it. Paul means the same: the
body is dead on account of sin, the Spirit is life. The "sinful
flesh", the seat of the opposition-government against God, is
rendered powerless, in that Christ has us in his power through
his Spirit. As sin and death belong together, so also do righteousness and life. What is as yet only an intimation, that which
is still in the balance, will one day be a final decree. We shall
be partakers of eternal life with Christ and through him. But
that no hostile attitude to the body is being proclaimed here,
as in Greek thought where the body is made responsible for

death and sin, is shown in the reference to the resurrection of
the body. As Christ Himself is risen bodily, not merely spiritu-
ally, so we too shall experience the raising of the body. The
Spirit is not separated from the body, but God's Spirit who
dwells in us, becomes in God's hand the means towards a new
quickening of the body. Therefore the Spirit, who has now
made his abode in the Christian, is the connecting link between
the present and future existence, or, as Paul expresses it at
another place, the "pledge" of eternal glory. In fact, he who
has received the Holy Ghost "has eternal life".

[12]So then, brethren, we are debtors, not to the flesh, to live
according to the flesh—[13]for if you live according to the flesh
you will die, but if by the Spirit you put to death the deeds of
the body you will live. [14]For all who are led by the Spirit of God
are sons of God. [15]For you did not receive the spirit of slavery
to fall back into fear, but you have received the spirit of sonship. When we cry, "Abba! Father!" [16]it is the Spirit himself
bearing witness with our spirit that we are children of God,
[17]and if children, then heirs, heirs of God and fellow heirs with
Christ, provided we suffer with him in order that we may also
be glorified with him.

The life in Christ is a new reality, not a mere idea, or an ideal
or standard. But here again, as in the sixth chapter, Paul has
to remind us that this new reality must prove itself in a new
willing; yes, even in a new "owing". Possessing the Spirit is at
the same time a fresh obligation to be loyal to the Spirit. Once
more the wild thought ought to be dismissed that the new life
is realized by a kind of natural necessity, that it comes off
without a struggle. On the contrary, it is a life and death
struggle. You are to kill the impulses of the flesh, the "deeds of
the body". We shall see later (12: 1ff.) that Paul does not
intend by this an ethic of the ascetic negation of life. We have
already heard that it concerns the using of the members of the
body as God's instruments for God's war. By the deeds of the
body is meant therefore the leaderless self-activity of the sinful
flesh, the result of a freedom from restraint. That belongs to
the old nature and can only nourish the fear of death. "For he
who sows to his own flesh will from the flesh reap corruption,

but he who sows to the Spirit will from the Spirit reap eternal
life" (Gal. 6: 8).

The Christian man is not leaderless but a man who is led.
The Spirit is not only the liberator but also the leader. The
characteristic of the sons of God is that they are under the
guidance of the Holy Spirit. We ought not to translate with
Luther "driven by the Spirit" but "led by the Spirit". As we
see from the first letter to the Corinthians, the distinctive mark
of Christians is that they are no longer "driven", like the
heathen, but led. Thus the Holy Spirit is distinguished from
any kind of fanaticism (*Schwärmerei*).

And now the great word is spoken: Sons of God, children of
God. The apostle uses both expressions side by side, the one as
signifying the new dignity, the other as an indication of our
dependence on God. The characteristic sign of divine Sonship
is guidance by the Holy Spirit; "adoption", elevation to the
filial status through God's decree and will is its basis. Once
more, though only by a hint, we are reminded of the Law.
Whoever is under the Law is a slave (Gal. 4: 1-7) and is
governed by fear; whoever is under the guidance of the Spirit
is a son and is ruled by love and trust in the Father who
acknowledges him as his son and child.

The two main themes of the letter to the Romans are
summed up here in one concept: Spirit of sonship; more precisely, Spirit of the acknowledgment of sonship; we may also
translate it, Spirit of justifying grace. For the acknowledgment
of sonship is, indeed, only a new word for that which elsewhere
is called "justification by faith alone". Where the answer Yes
is given to God's judgment of justification, where man allows
it to be said to himself, accepting it in hearty faith that God
acknowledges him as son, there the Holy Spirit is operative.
The apostle says both things: We cry, "Abba! Father!" and
the Spirit cries it, too (Gal. 4: 6). Indeed, he also unifies the
two: the Spirit testifies together with our spirit that we are
children of God. The inherence of what the Holy Spirit cries
and what we cry, and yet the distinction between them, is
something final, indescribable and incomprehensible. "It is
no longer I who live but Christ who lives in me" (Gal. 2: 20).

Here one might perhaps speak of faith mysticism or Christ
mysticism. Even the sober Calvin uses the phrase *unio mystica*

for this highest and final thing. One might or one might not! What Paul means has only a very remote resemblance to what is generally called mysticism. For here we are concerned with justifying faith in the Son, the Mediator who has become incarnate. It is a question of sonship, not a mutual inter-mixing of God and man. It is a question of an experience which must work itself out in a sober obedience and a hard struggle, nay, which only is real at all in such a struggle. It is not a question of an experience of one-ness but of an act of trust. Of course, that distance between God and man which arouses fear is eliminated here; it belongs to slavery, not to sonship, to being under the Law, not to life in the Spirit. "There is no fear in love", says John; fear can no longer exist where one cries "Father", says Paul.

Another distance, however, does continue to exist, namely the one between the now and the hereafter. We are still only adopted; we have not yet taken over the inheritance. We have been appointed heirs apparent of eternal life and its fulfilment, but we do not yet enjoy it. We have the full assurance of future glory, but we are not yet out of the life where there is fighting and suffering. Indeed, a definite suffering actually belongs to true discipleship. Whoever does not take up his own cross and follow him, cannot be his disciple (Matt. 16: 24). He who does not want to suffer with Christ cannot share in his glory either. The way of the Christian is not a path on the heights but down below. The way on the heights is in heaven, not on earth—or on earth only where one knows nothing of Christ, the Crucified.

THE NEW HOPE (8: 18-30)

[18]I consider that the sufferings of this present time are not worth comparing with the glory that is to be revealed to us. [19]For the creation waits with eager longing for the revealing of the sons of God; [20]for the creation was subjected to futility, not of its own will but by the will of him who subjected it in hope; [21]because the creation itself will be set free from its bondage to decay and obtain the glorious liberty of the children of God. [22]We know that the whole creation has been groaning in travail together until now; [23]and not only the creation, but we ourselves, who have the first fruits of the Spirit, groan inwardly

73

as we wait for adoption as sons, the redemption of our bodies.
²⁴For in this hope we were saved. Now hope that is seen is not
hope. For who hopes for what he sees? ²⁵But if we hope for what
we do not see, we wait for it with patience.

²⁶Likewise the Spirit helps us in our weakness; for we do not
know how to pray as we ought, but the Spirit himself intercedes for us with sighs too deep for words. ²⁷And he who
searches the hearts of men knows what is the mind of the
Spirit, because the Spirit intercedes for the saints according
to the will of God.

²⁸We know that in everything God works for good with those
who love him, who are called according to his purpose. ²⁹For
those whom he foreknew he also predestined to be conformed
to the image of his Son, in order that he might be the firstborn
among many brethren. ³⁰And those whom he predestined he
also called; and those whom he called he also justified; and
those whom he justified he also glorified.

The Christian status has, like human life in general, three
temporal dimensions: past, present and future. It is based on
the foundation that is laid, Christ (1 Cor. 3: 11), it lives in the
present of the Spirit, it reaches out towards full redemption in
the future. After having thoroughly dealt with the first two,
Paul now turns to the third, the hope given us in Christ. With
the thought that as sons we are also heirs, the link is forged
between present and future, between faith and hope. This
glimpse into the future glory forms a sharp contrast to the
present reality, to this world full of suffering, in the very midst
of which we also as Christians still stand. But how insignificant
this is now! The glory of which we are certain makes our sufferings appear of little importance.

On the other hand we can only look in faith on the present
as something preliminary, on what has been created as something advancing towards a goal. Paul chiefly thinks, at that
point, of mankind; it is subjected to futility, it awaits the
revelation of the sons of God. We stand again before the
thought of the fifth chapter. All mankind was dragged by
Adam's transgression into the state of death; therefore it longs
for and awaits redemption. This state of subjection to the power
of corruption is expressly distinguished from that which
derives from man's own will; it is a fate which we suffer in

74

common. No one is asked. On the other hand this expectation of the creature is distinct from the hope of Christians. It is an apathetic, unconscious waiting, a waiting for something better, yet uncertain of its goal. But it is expounded by the apostle according to its true nature. What men actually mean without knowing it, is the goal which in Christ has been given to mankind; divine sonship, freedom, divine adoption, participation in the glory of God.

To what extent Paul is also thinking here of the sub-human creation it is hard to say. The expression "the whole creation", "all that is created", certainly seems to suggest this, so that the phrase has been mostly understood in this way. On the other hand one cannot fail to recognize that this concept "creation" mostly denotes humanity for Paul, and that he nowhere else speaks of the world of nature. That the whole world has been dragged into the corruption brought about by Adam's fall is an idea which may have been familiar to the apostle from the rabbinical tradition. It is therefore not impossible that that thought is also included here. Suffering in the sub-human creation is a fact one can hardly overlook, and it is a great enigma for us. That this suffering may be conditioned by something which has happened to and through man has become for us to-day a scarcely feasible thought, since we know to-day quite definitely of a natural history preceding the history of man by hundreds or thousands of million years, a natural history with the same cruel struggle for existence and terrible catastrophes as they are known to us from present-day Nature. We approach here a boundary not of our own understanding but of biblical teaching.

This sighing, which can be heard throughout the whole of creation, be it human or sub-human, is also our lot as Christians. We are indeed redeemed by Jesus Christ—the usual distinction drawn by theologians between reconciliation as something already accomplished and redemption as something that is only to take place in the future is unknown to Paul, as well as to the whole of the Bible. Of course, we have already become sons or children of God; but the effect of the redemption and the full realization of sonship is still outstanding. We have only the first fruits of the Spirit, the pledge of life in the glory of God, but this glory itself in its fulness is not yet here.

We hope for it. In declaring that hope belongs to the Christian status just as love and faith do, we also say we have not everything yet but only wait for the whole.

This becomes particularly clear when thinking of our physical life. Again Paul contrasts with one another Spirit (the Holy Spirit) and body, the body weighed down by sin and therefore mortal. "This body of death" is in fact the most massive sign of redemption not yet happened but only expected and hoped for. Nevertheless one must not, as might be possible linguistically, understand Paul as if he means "redemption from the body". Yes, he has expressly said redemption from the body of this death (7: 24), but equally explicitly he has spoken of the certain hope that God "will give life to your mortal bodies", by letting the raising of Jesus also happen to us. Paul thus wants to say that, as long as we are joined to this mortal body burdened with sin and weakness, we know that our redemption has only begun and that we should await its fulfilment with patience but also with glad certainty.

The weakness, however, does not refer merely to our body; it penetrates to the innermost being, into the life of prayer. We cannot even pray as we really ought to. It simply will not do to say that the Lord has given us in the Lord's Prayer the example of true prayer valid for all time. Prayer should also, as we see from the letters of the apostle, bring before God the daily needs and requirements of individuals and communities. And now it is demonstrated just here at the centre of the Christian life that "our knowledge is imperfect" (1 Cor. 13: 9). We surely often pray wrongly because we do not know ourselves what is good for our true salvation and that of others. But, says Paul, that is not really important if only God's Spirit does truly dwell in us. Then something of the Holy Spirit accompanies it, so to speak, in and under our prayer which is not of us but of him, a thing truly pleasing to God; yes, one may say, a divine groaning without words, which God understands since it comes from God. Thus not only do all living creatures groan, not only do Christians, but even the Holy Ghost that dwells in us; the Spirit of God Himself groans in us, with us, for us, also above us, we may be sure. It is something tremendous that God Himself as the Holy Spirit dwelling in us also groans. Truly, this God is not "the Absolute", "the Supreme Being" of whom the philosophers speak, and to whom (and with them so many theologians of old time) they have to ascribe an absolute impassibility!

But God helps us, not only by this innermost assistance of the Holy Spirit in our prayer, but through everything that happens to us. That is the impenetrable mystery of the divine ruling of the world: that all conditions and events of life are in his hand, bringing us to our goal. Of course, by this no universal world optimism is meant—everything will turn out all right for everybody in any case. There stands here the significant limitation, "to those who love God". Paul thus speaks here of the community of Christians, the believers. Therefore it depends on us, for is it not our love to God, our faith which decides whether we reach our goal? Paul denies this question, not merely in order to humble us, but equally to give us a firm position. Those who love God are, of course, those who are called according to God's decree. And now Paul creates that "golden chain" of concepts which link both ends of the path of salvation: Election-pre-destination-calling-justification-glorification. In these five words we have been given a "sum of theology", a summary of all Christian doctrine.

The next chapter will deal in detail with election. It is the beginning of everything. God's thought, God's will is the absolute priority. That God has "chosen" a creation is the reason why created things exist; that God has chosen us men as his creaturely image is the ground for our existence as men; that God has loved us from eternity in Jesus Christ is the ground for our salvation. Paul links predestination with the thought of the image of God. The image of God's Son is God's plan for humanity; to become like him is the final goal of mankind. In the God-Man, Jesus Christ, has not only been made manifest to us who God is, but also what man is and ought to become according to his true nature. Jesus Christ, the risen Christ, is "the first true man"; for Paul speaks of him as only "the firstborn among many brothers". This predestination is realized only through the Word, God's call to every in-dividual. Chapter 10 will have more to say on this. God's call is made through the special messengers of God, the prophets and apostles and all who proclaim his message. "Called to be saints"—that is Paul's usual mode of address to his fellow

Christians, i.e., they are those who through God's call are set apart from the rest of the world to be the peculiar people of God. The contents of this message and call is the grace granted by God, justification by faith. It is also, as we have seen, the basis of life for the Christian and the Christian Community. But it, too, has not reached the goal; justification is only the sure promise of eternal life, of eternal glory; yet it is not itself that.

But it is the goal beyond which nothing higher can be thought of, nor has been promised. The glorification of God in the glorification of man, man's full participation in the eternally blessed life of God through God's gift, full communion with God and thus with one another which is no longer clouded by any sin and death—that is the content of the hope of salvation which is given to us in Jesus Christ.

THE ASSURANCE OF REDEMPTION (8: 31-39)

[31]What then shall we say to this? If God is for us, who is against us? [32]He who did not spare his own Son but gave him up for us all, will he not also give us all things with him? [33]Who shall bring any charge against God's elect? It is God who justifies; [34]who is to condemn? Is it Christ Jesus, who died, yes, who was raised from the dead, who is at the right hand of God, who indeed intercedes for us? [35]Who shall separate us from the love of Christ? Shall tribulation, or distress, or persecution, or famine, or nakedness, or peril, or sword? [36]As it is written,

> "For thy sake we are being killed all the day long;
> we are regarded as sheep to be slaughtered."

[37]No, in all these things we are more than conquerors through him who loved us. [38]For I am sure that neither death, nor life, nor angels, nor principalities, nor things present, nor things to come, nor powers, [39]nor height, nor depth, nor anything else in all creation, will be able to separate us from the love of God in Christ Jesus our Lord.

The first main object of the letter has been attained. The Roman Community knows now what kind of message the apostle to the Gentiles has to declare to them as well as to the entire world, and what every Christian has received through

God acting in Jesus Christ. Yet Paul as a good teacher again wants to summarize the main point. But what a teacher this witness to salvation is! With what a triumphant authority of the Spirit he knows how to express, in a few words, what the Christian life is all about! God is for us; that is the salvation against which everything "in opposition" does not prevail. God is for us; the Gentile does not know this, nor even the Jew; they are not acquainted with this assurance as the power determining the whole of life. This joy and assurance are the contents of the glad tidings of Jesus Christ. If God so loves us that he gives for us his most beloved and his very own, his Son, then everything else need no longer worry us. He who gave us the greatest thing will also not deny us the smaller.

God is for us. Others, of course, have already said that, for instance Gentile nations who went to war trusting in the special assistance of their national god. They will go on saying this in the future when it is a question of procuring divine blessing for specific human wishes and aims. Yet in their hearts dwells anxiety, in their secret hours they are tortured by the consciousness of guilt, unable to overcome the fear of death. If the cry "God for us" is to become true a change must be brought about at the centre of human life. The accusation which is "against us" must be removed. It is removed by God, who justifies the sinner in Jesus Christ.

"The greatest among evils is guilt". That the Gentiles also knew, somehow; every man dully perceives it without knowing it. That is the wrath of God which is revealed in regard to all unrighteousness of men. This main evil is eliminated; the accusation against us is swallowed up in the reconciling death of the Son of God. The great enemy has been vanquished at the very point where he reckoned on securing his main triumph. For the Crucified is the risen Lord; he who died with the words "My God, my God, why hast thou forsaken me" on his lips, sits now at the right hand of God. He is the victor over death and hell. God for us means now: "God is love". What has come to us in Jesus Christ? Answer: God's love in spite of sin and guilt. The love of Jesus is the love of God, the love of God is that which Jesus Christ has brought to us who are afraid of God because of sin and grants to everyone who believes in him.

Will that continue to remain so? Does the love of Jesus

prevail against all the dark forces which have power in our life? Can one believe in the love of God in the face of everything that men have had to go through in this world and must continue to go through again and again? For things after all do not happen to us in the way in which many are inclined to understand verse 28, as a beautiful saying that for Christians in their earthly days things will be better than for others. That this certainly cannot be the case, Paul has explained to us in the eleventh chapter of the second letter to the Corinthians, where he tells us what he, as Jesus' apostle, had to go through; so that one cries in astonishment: What an exceptional man he is, able to endure all that! In reality: tribulation, distress, persecution, famine, nakedness, peril and sword. All this Paul experienced more than once. He thus knows what he is talking about when speaking of these things.

It is Paul then, if anyone, who knows that being joined to Christ does not make life any easier, that it does not remove from life, but rather increases what men point to everywhere when they want to show why they cannot believe in a loving God. And, like him, many thousands of other faithful witnesses of Christ have experienced it throughout all the centuries until our own time, the time of fresh persecutions of Christians. Yet the apostle is not surprised at it. The disciple is not above his Master. If they have crucified him, if his life was suffering, why should it be any better for his disciples? If God was able through the suffering of Christ to give the world proof of his love, then the suffering of Christians cannot obscure this love in the slightest. "In all these things we are more than conquerors"; for there is one thing of which they cannot be deprived, namely, the union with him who is love, the daily new experience of this love amidst all trouble and distress. The Gospel is a message of triumph, not only in view of the end, but already in view of the experience of the Christian Community. The life in the Holy Spirit is no longer that lamentable swaying to and fro between victory and defeat which characterizes the condition of man under the Law; it is a victorious life. Paul uses here a strong and untranslatable expression. We are "excessively victorious". The joy of victory is the sign of the life in the Spirit in the same way as the wretched sinfulness is the mark of legalism. It is true that whoever truly belongs to Christ never leaves the groaning behind, as long as he lives on earth, but he does leave the moaning and anxiety. The note of victory is the visible mark of those who are united with the victor.

For I am *sure*—that is the test of invincibility. On this depends nothing less than everything. Even the most glorious experiences, the most convincing theological trains of thought, the most striking biblical proofs, the grandest and deepest spiritual outlooks do not help if you are not sure of your faith. And the lack of all this is ultimately not harmful if nevertheless you are sure of your salvation in Christ and of the love of God. The assurance is what matters; everything depends on it. There are no proofs that God is love. Still less is there any proof that he loves you. He has revealed himself in Jesus Christ, he has revealed himself in this way in his Word, he addresses you in this way right through all contrary experience in the world. But everything depends on whether you are sure of it. No one else can take your place; this assurance you must already possess completely for yourself. Others can testify to you of their assurance and strengthen you with it, or perhaps not. In any case the main thing is whether you are certain of it. And that is the only "proof" of the truth of Christ's message: the strength of the assurance that becomes effective as the power of a new life.

This assurance is not automatic; it has to fight its way through against powerful opposing forces. Natural and supernatural powers threaten it. Demonic powers continually try to talk us out of faith in God's love; to ridicule it, to cast doubts on it as an untenable superstition. Indeed, Paul is perhaps also thinking here of a spiritual struggle, invisible to us and not entering into our experience, between such supernatural powers and Christ Himself (1 Cor. 15: 24). But whatever adversaries assail us and our faith, one thing they cannot do: separate us from Christ, make obscure and incredible the love of God which we have known in Christ. What Paul has taught us in these eight chapters is not a beautiful theory but an experience tried in the fiery trial of suffering and struggle.

Part Two

THE RIGHTEOUSNESS OF GOD IN HIS RULING OF HISTORY (9: 1—11: 36)

THE PAINFUL RIDDLE OF ISRAEL (9: 1-5)

¹I am speaking the truth in Christ, I am not lying; my conscience bears me witness in the Holy Spirit, ²that I have great sorrow and unceasing anguish in my heart. ³For I could wish that I myself were accursed and cut off from Christ for the sake of my brethren, my kinsmen by race. ⁴They are Israelites, and to them belong the sonship, the glory, the covenants, the giving of the law, the worship, and the promises; ⁵to them belong the patriarchs, and of their race, according to the flesh, is the Christ. God who is over all be blessed for ever. Amen.

WITHOUT transition but with a sudden change, the shout of joy with which the first main part of the letter came to an end is followed by this deeply moving complaint at the beginning of the second. For we are still in the flesh which, as long as it lives, must groan even though God's Spirit rejoices in it. Yet this groaning, too, is no mere outbreak of a natural feeling; it is of the same kind as: "He had compassion on the multitude" (Matt. 9: 36). The apostle laments over his people; he bears with his brothers their misery as a loyal fellow-countryman who, in spite of his separation brought about through Christ, feels himself so united with them that he would gladly surrender his own happiness if he could thereby save his people. But it is not only a blood relationship or a historical one. He feels within himself the conflict between the present spiritual condition of Israel and its divine history. The heritage of Israel! The first question is answered as to how the Law entrusted to the Jews is related to the new gift, the salvation in Christ. But there remains still the other question: namely, what is to be the future destiny of the nation itself to whom this inheritance was entrusted and which, after all, rejected Christ. With this question Paul wrestles in the next three chapters.

83

Israel's riddle is no mere historical question. That the people with the promises could be rejected—that is a thought all the more distressing in that Christ Himself is descended from this people. As Israel possessed in the Holy of Holies of the Temple something of God's glorious presence, so is he, in whom the eternal God Himself became man as an Israelite born, a new proof of the particular intentions of God with this nation. And yet it rejected him.

THE FREEDOM OF GOD (9: 6-29)

[6]But it is not as though the word of God had failed. For not all who are descended from Israel belong to Israel, [7]and not all are children of Abraham because they are his descendants; but "Through Isaac shall your descendants be named." [8]This means that it is not the children of the flesh who are the children of God, but the children of the promise are reckoned as descendants. [9]For this is what the promise said, "About this time I will return and Sarah shall have a son." [10]And not only so, but also when Rebecca had conceived children by one man, our forefather Isaac, [11]though they were not yet born and had done nothing either good or bad, in order that God's purpose of election might continue, not because of works but because of his call, [12]she was told, "The elder will serve the younger." [13]As it is written, "Jacob I loved, but Esau I hated."

What is peculiar and unique in regard to Israel is the fact that a divine history is embedded in its natural history as a people. There is thus always a double Israel: an Israel in the sense of nature and secular history and an Israel in the sense of divine history. How much these two diverge becomes especially clear to the apostle in the history of Abraham and Jacob, the two patriarchs.

In both there is an intersection of the divine history and the natural. Both are thus witnesses to God's freedom, who intervenes in secular history as he wills, separating to himself a people by election, cutting right across all natural blood relationships. Not only natural descent according to blood but also moral qualities show that they have no validity here. The divine history has its basis solely in God's decree. This does not mean that physical descent, the natural unity of the people and Israel's history are unimportant; it is merely intended to show that God can do with it what he wills, that he is not bound to it, and the Jew cannot derive from it any rights. But one can as little deduce from the example of Jacob and Esau a double decree of God which from eternity has decreed one for damnation and the other to everlasting life. It is not talking about this here but about God's freedom to cut across natural ties, according to his choice, through his history of redemption. That the history of redemption runs through Jacob and not Esau is God's free act; there is no word here regarding the bliss or wretchedness of Jacob and Esau. But when Paul quotes the saying of the prophet Malachi that God hated Esau, then he is certainly not forgetting that "Esau" there stands for the people of Edom, who because of their "wickedness" were overtaken by God's righteous judgment. That is also the case in what follows.

[14]What shall we say then? Is there injustice on God's part? By no means! [15]For he says to Moses, "I will have mercy on whom I have mercy, and I will have compassion on whom I have compassion." [16]So it depends not upon man's will or exertion, but upon God's mercy. [17]For the scripture says to Pharaoh, "I have raised you up for the very purpose of showing my power in you, so that my name may be proclaimed in all the earth." [18]So then he has mercy upon whomever he wills, and he hardens the heart of whomever he wills.

[19]You will say to me then, "Why does he still find fault? For who can resist his will?" [20]But, who are you, a man, to answer back to God? Will what is moulded say to its moulder, "Why have you made me thus?" [21]Has the potter no right over the clay, to make out of the same lump one vessel for beauty and another for menial use? [22]What if God, desiring to show his wrath and to make known his power, has endured with much patience the vessels of wrath made for destruction, [23]in order to make known the riches of his glory for the vessels of mercy, which he has prepared beforehand for glory, [24]even us whom he has called, not from the Jews only but also from the Gentiles? [25]As indeed he says in Hosea,

"Those who were not my people
I will call 'my people,'
and her who was not beloved
I will call 'my beloved.' "
[26]"And in the very place where it was

said to them, 'You are not my
people,'
they will be called 'sons of the living
God.' "
[27]And Isaiah cries out concerning Israel: "Though the
number of the sons of Israel be as the sand of the sea, only a
remnant of them will be saved; [28]for the Lord will execute his
sentence upon the earth with rigor and dispatch." [29]And as
Isaiah predicted,
"If the Lord of hosts had not left us children,
we would have fared like Sodom and been made like
Gomorrah."

God's freedom means inequality. Inequality, however,
always arouses in us men the feeling of injustice. We want to
measure God by our yardstick. But God's righteousness
cannot be measured by our standards. It includes his absolute
sovereign freedom; else he would not be the God who freely
bestows. His giving is subject to no rule but his will alone.

He thus grants his mercy to whom he wills. No one has a
right to his mercy; there is no possibility of gaining it. God's
mercy is a free gift. Yet God also hardens whom he wills. What
the nature of his hardening is he shows us in Pharaoh. He
hardens the man who rebels against him. In this, too—that is
the secret of his omnipotence—he asserts his will and his
honour. The parallel with Israel is already hinted at here. Even
though he rejects Israel because it opposes him, it must serve
his plan for the world and the spreading of his honour.

But now human reason revolts more than ever. If God acts
thus, where is human guilt? If after all everything is in God's
hand, where is our responsibility? Human thought never does
reconcile God's freedom and our responsibility. Yet Paul will
not allow himself to be enticed into philosophical paths. Whoever cannot bear the thought that God is the absolutely free
Lord forgets that he is a creature, who is placing himself on
the same level with the Creator. Therefore, it must first be
shown to him again in as obvious a manner as possible who he
is: a creature, i.e. a nobody apart from God's will and work. If
God is the Creator, who is to give him orders about what he
has to do? God can do what he wills, just as the potter can
make ornamental vessels and chamber-pots. "As little as the

clay guides the hand of the potter at his work, so little does a man compel God to give" (Schlatter).

The metaphor must not be pressed; God is not a potter and man is not a lump of clay. Thus Paul does not want to say that God has made men as vessels of wrath. He is speaking of Israel, and God has certainly not made Israel for wrath. But by its disobedience—as we see in the tenth chapter—Israel has become a vessel of God's wrath. To be sure, God will not only be gracious but as the Holy One will also exercise judgment. Whoever has fallen under his wrath through disobedience, him he prepares for destruction. "Ready for destruction" does not, however, mean "made for destruction", and being a vessel of wrath does not imply having been made in or for wrath. It is a misplaced logic to refer back at this point to the sentence which deals with Esau, and concludes that there are those whom God hates from eternity and whom he made for destruction out of hatred and in wrath. By connecting up his thoughts in such a way violence is done to what Paul means to convey. He only wants to say: nobody has a right to God's grace, least of all they who through disobedience have fallen under God's wrath. If God still spares even those who are approaching their judgment then it shows his forbearance—the forbearance that is to lead to repentance (2: 4)—and this, too, serves for the carrying out of his plan of salvation. Of a double decree (predestination), one leading to eternal life and the other to eternal damnation, this passage teaches just as little as any other part of Holy Scripture.

It does teach, however, less ambiguously and more bluntly than any other, the absolute sovereign right of God and the futility of all human claims on God's grace. If God grants his mercy, there was nothing that obliged him to do so, and whether he wants to do it man cannot deduce from any concept of God. And finally: if God shows mercy, then man's will and achievement cannot claim the least little part in it. It is God's act alone.

The entire chapter, however, like the two following, concerns the riddle of Israel. God is free to reject Israel because of its unbelief without therefore becoming unfaithful to his promise. For his promise does not refer to Israel as a natural community of people but to the spiritual Israel that certainly has its beginning within the history of the people of Israel. That is the meaning of the Old Testament quotation in verses 25-29. God remains faithful to his promise given to Israel, even though he rejects the unbelieving Israel; for he forms to himself an obedient Israel out of Jews and Gentiles upon whom he fulfils his decree of salvation. Thus the connection is restored with the thoughts which he has already worked out in the second and fourth chapters, and which clarify the main theme of the letter: the righteousness of God. It concerns the righteousness which God bestows, not the kind that man believes he has of himself; it concerns free mercy and not human claims. The fact that the Jews do not wish to understand it is precisely their ruin.

THE UNBELIEF OF ISRAEL (9: 30—10: 21)

The Self-righteousness of Israel (9: 30—10: 3)

³⁰What shall we say, then? That Gentiles who did not pursue righteousness have attained it, that is, righteousness through faith; ³¹but that Israel who pursued the righteousness which is based on law did not succeed in fulfilling that law. ³²Why? Because they did not pursue it through faith, but as if it were based on works. They have stumbled over the stumbling stone, ³³as it is written,

"Behold I am laying in Zion a stone that will make men stumble,

a rock that will make them fall; and he who believes in him will not be put to shame."

10. ¹Brethren, my heart's desire and prayer to God for them is that they may be saved. ²I bear them witness that they have a zeal for God, but it is not enlightened. ³For, being ignorant of the righteousness that comes from God, and seeking to establish their own, they did not submit to God's righteousness.

God's freedom is shown by things turning out so very differently from what man would have thought. The great example of this is the history of the message of salvation among the Jews and the Gentiles. The Jews, by their divine preparation the first candidates for Christ's salvation, have not obtained it and the Gentile nations, who knew nothing of it whatever, have received it. Those who strove hard went away empty and those who did not strive at all won it.

Why is that? The answer which Paul gives to this decisive question shows how far from him lay the doctrine of the double decree, on behalf of which one has so often appealed to him. The answer does not run: The reason just lies in the mysterious decree of God, who predestines some to salvation and others to damnation. It reads: It is the consequence of the Jews wanting to be righteous of themselves, and therefore they had turned a deaf ear to the message of the freely bestowed righteousness of God. The message of God's righteousness in Jesus Christ became for them that stumbling stone and rock of offence of which Isaiah speaks. It is not one's own righteousness which decides, but faith; that is, the readiness to allow oneself to be given salvation by God.

Yet Paul simply cannot rest content with this knowledge. The fate of his people affects him too closely for the question to be settled for him with the knowledge of the reason for their rejection. He has to wrestle with it again from the beginning. Two things he cannot shake himself free from: he loves his people with his whole heart, and he respects their earnest striving for righteousness. He is certainly not one of those newly converted who, because of their life having undergone a break and an abrupt change, deny and blacken their past. His love for his people has not grown cold in the least; he would pawn his own happiness for them. And even the legal righteousness in which he was brought up does not simply mean nothing to him. He wants explicitly to testify that they have zeal for God. The verdict here, at any rate apparently, sounds milder than in the second and third chapters; for he speaks only as a man, measuring with human standards. Who would deny that with regard to morality the Jewish people of his time surpassed all other nations? But it is precisely that which becomes a snare for them. They are the "righteous ones who have no need of repentance", they believe they are able to stand and exist in their own righteousness before God. Therefore they do not need him who came to call sinners to repentance and in whom God grants his salvation as a gift. They do not want it as a gift; thus they do not wish to believe. With all their knowledge of God they just remain closed against what matters most, the message from the God who freely gives. This is the content of the next section.

The True Way of Salvation (10: 4-15)

⁴For Christ is the end of the law, that every one who has faith may be justified.

⁵Moses writes that the man who practises the righteousness which is based on the law shall live by it. ⁶But the righteousness based on faith says, Do not say in your heart, "Who will ascend into heaven?" (that is, to bring Christ down) ⁷or "Who will descend into the abyss?" (that is, to bring Christ up from the dead). ⁸But what does it say? The word is near you, on your lips and in your heart (that is, the word of faith which we preach); ⁹because, if you confess with your lips that Jesus is Lord and believe in your heart that God raised him from the dead, you will be saved. ¹⁰For man believes with his heart and so is justified, and he confesses with his lips and so is saved. ¹¹The scripture says, "No one who believes in him will be put to shame." ¹²For there is no distinction between Jew and Greek; the same Lord is Lord of all and bestows his riches upon all who call upon him. ¹³For, "every one who calls upon the name of the Lord will be saved."

¹⁴But how are men to call upon him in whom they have not believed? And how are they to believe in him of whom they have never heard? And how are they to hear without a preacher? ¹⁵And how can men preach unless they are sent? As it is written, "How beautiful are the feet of those who preach good news!"

Once more the two ways which are the main theme of the letter are opposed: The way of the Law and the way of faith. Whoever wanted to reach the goal along the path of the Law would have to fulfil the Law. That this is useless Paul believes he has sufficiently demonstrated by this time. In Christ this way has come to its end. Since him and through him one is able to know that it does not lead to the goal. But just there the new way is also opened up which leads to the goal: it is the righteousness by faith, the fellowship with God as granted, not gained, from the beginning. It is now no longer a question of bringing down righteousness from above or bringing it up from below— the way of all human religion—but it is here in the Word of Christ and in faith in Christ.

Paul now demonstrates this new way of salvation in a chain of ideas which leads backwards from present faith to the origin of the whole movement. Salvation is here, on your lips—by

your confession—and in your hearts—by faith. Out of the
heart faith rises to the lips as confession; faith is incomplete if
it does not become audible in witness. The confession of faith
before the world is in this world the end of the line—as it also
again becomes the beginning. For how does faith enter into the
heart? Through hearing. And how can it be heard except
by preaching, how could they preach without being sent? The
commission which is linked to the gift does not allow the
movement to come to a standstill. Where faith is, there is the
mandate to confess. But where confession is, there preaching
takes place, from which faith emerges once again. As the
substance of faith and the message is God's self-communicating
love, so the self-communication of faith is once more its natural
movement forward. Faith comes from other men and leads to
other men. Faith comes from outside and leads to outside; it
springs from "verbal declaration," as Luther always emphasized, and leads to verbal declaration. As faith has as its object
an historical event, the Christ-event, so it also expands in an
historical form and again creates history. Faith and mission are
inseparably linked.

The Disobedience of Israel (10: 16-21)

16But they have not all heeded the gospel; for Isaiah says,
"Lord, who has believed what he has heard from us?" 17So
faith comes from what is heard, and what is heard comes by the
preaching of Christ.
18But I ask, have they not heard? Indeed they have; for
"Their voice has gone out to all the earth,
and their word to the ends of the world."
19Again I ask, did Israel not understand? First Moses says,
"I will make you jealous of those who are not a nation;
with a foolish nation I will make you angry."
20Then Isaiah is so bold as to say,
"I have been found by those who did not seek me;
I have shown myself to those who did not ask for me."
21But of Israel he says, "All day long I have held out my
hands to a disobedient and contrary people."

What has happened then to Israel? How is one to understand the riddle of the Jewish people? The answer can only

run: The riddle of Israel is the riddle of disobedience, of un-belief towards God's bestowing Word. The Greek words of the apostle cannot be adequately translated at the crucial point. He forms three main concepts from the root of one word. Obedience, hearing and "what is heard"; we speak of a "vision of Isaiah", the apostle speaks essentially of "what is heard". This "thing that is heard" is at the same time a message. Faith thus comes in a double sense from "what is heard": From the message which itself is "something heard"—and from hearing the message. And this act of hearing is both times obedience. If instead of "what is heard" we translate it by preaching, not only is Paul's play on words lost but, what is more important still, the actual sense of the whole chapter: the fact that hearing, obedience, faith and proclamation belong together; also both ends of the chain which form a pair: making one's faith known through confession and the hearing of the divine commission.

Israel cannot excuse itself. There was no lack of publishing the message; there was also no deficiency of intelligibility. If the Gentiles have understood, how should not the Jews have been able even more to understand it! They did not want to understand; they were disobedient. But how little Paul is inclined even here to trace back human disobedience to an eternal divine decree of hardening is shown in the last of his quotations: God truly has not failed in providing proofs of his seeking love. As a mother runs after her disobedient child to entice him home, so God has stretched out his hands towards Israel—but in vain. Why? Because Israel did not want to. That is the final answer. Paul, at all events, no longer looks for an answer behind it in the hidden will of God. This is made perfectly clear in the next chapter.

THE FAITHFULNESS OF GOD IS GREATER THAN THE UNFAITHFULNESS OF MAN (11: 1-36)

The Israel of Faith (11: 1-10)

[1]I ask, then, has God rejected his people? By no means! I myself am an Israelite, a descendant of Abraham, a member of the tribe of Benjamin. [2]God has not rejected his people whom he foreknew. Do you not know what the scripture says of Elijah, how he pleads with God against Israel? [3]"Lord, they have killed thy prophets, they have demolished thy altars,

and I alone am left, and they seek my life." ⁴But what is God's reply to him? "I have kept for myself seven thousand men who have not bowed the knee to Baal." ⁵So too at the present time there is a remnant, chosen by grace. ⁶But if it is by grace, it is no longer on the basis of works; otherwise grace would no longer be grace.

⁷What then? Israel failed to obtain what it sought. The elect obtained it, but the rest were hardened, ⁸as it is written,

"God gave them a spirit of stupor,
eyes that should not see and ears that should not hear,
down to this very day."

⁹And David says,

"Let their feast become a snare and a trap,
a pitfall and a retribution for them;
¹⁰let their eyes be darkened so that they cannot see,
and bend their backs for ever."

The question of Israel's destiny is now clarified by the past; we know now why things have turned out in this way. The blame rests on their disobedience. But what is to happen to them? Is there an answer to this question which is directed to the future? Paul dares to give it in this chapter. In doing so he becomes a prophet; he attempts to draw, at least in their most general features, the future ways of God with mankind and with Israel. This chapter is perhaps the most daring that Paul ever wrote. It is no accident that just he, the renegade who brought the salvation of the Jews to the Gentiles, whom the Jews therefore hated more than any other man, he whose whole thinking revolved round the contrast between Law and Gospel, had to write this prospect of the ultimate deliverance of the Jews; God had equipped him alone, this man in whose heart and life took place the whole argument about the difference between Judaism and the Christian Community.

Has God rejected Israel? No. The proving of this No is the substance of this chapter. First: Paul himself, of course, is an Israelite and that not only by blood but also because of the path along which he had deliberately walked. Thus he himself is the strongest evidence for the fact that saving grace can even subdue a fanatical advocate of the righteousness of the Law. Secondly: there is, of course, even in the Christian Community a selection of Jews.

93

The people as a whole are certainly disobedient; yet a remnant similar to that remnant of the faithful in the time of Elijah has received the Word of Christ. The apostle knows from his own experience that this is no merit. It is solely and simply the grace of God which gave this open ear. It is God's free choice, not a reward for human fulfilling of the Law. For the rest, the judgment of their disobedience is indeed fulfilled in their hardening. Hardening is being able no longer to say anything but No. God permits them to become entangled in their own No. The quotations from the Old Testament are meant to show that even where men turn their backs upon God, God is not, so to speak, disabled; there too he has his hand in the game. The hardening is as much his work as faith is. Just as God has given up the Gentiles "to the lust of their hearts" after their refusal to be drawn by him into true worship, so he now has also hardened the Jews after they have said their No. The hardening is not the original cause but God's punishment for their unbelief. Yet even that is not the last word.

The Wisdom of God uses also the Sin of Man (11: 11-24)

¹¹So I ask, have they stumbled so as to fall? By no means! But through their trespass salvation has come to the Gentiles, so as to make Israel jealous. ¹²Now if their trespass means riches for the world, and if their failure means riches for the Gentiles, how much more will their full inclusion mean!
¹³Now I am speaking to you Gentiles. Inasmuch then as I am an apostle to the Gentiles, I magnify my ministry ¹⁴in order to make my fellow Jews jealous, and thus save some of them. ¹⁵For if their rejection means the reconciliation of the world, what will their acceptance mean but life from the dead? ¹⁶If the dough offered as first fruits is holy, so is the whole lump; and if the root is holy, so are the branches.

The disobedience of Israel is a terrible fact. But the wisdom and omnipotence of God show themselves precisely at the point where his plan is apparently being crossed. The resistance of the Jews to Christ has become in God's hand the tool of reconciliation. What from man's side is called the Crucifixion of God's ambassador, that, from God's side, signifies the highest revelation of divine love. Thus the opposition of the Jews to

Christ's message made the apostle carry the Gospel into the world of the Gentiles. The Jews therefore went away empty-handed, yet it benefited the Gentiles. But if already the dis-obedience of the Jews had such a beneficial effect, what a blessing will their obedience in faith then be! When once the whole of Israel will have been converted to Christ the Lord, what a blessing that must be for the peoples of the world!

By way of the detour of the mission to the Gentiles, the Gospel will and must again return to the Jews. Once they see what the Gospel accomplishes among the Gentiles, they, too, will not be able to resist for long. Thus, at any rate, the apostle understands his mission and his service to the Gentiles. In this way he works, even though it be indirectly, for the conversion of his people. Only a Christian Community strong in faith and love can break the pride of the Jews and provoke them to emulation. But when that happens—Israel's conversion to Jesus Christ—then the fulness of his grace must come, the resurrection from the dead. Upon what is this daring hope based? What else but the divine promise? If God has chosen Israel, then he will also—even though it were through the midst of rejection and judgment—lead them to salvation. That which God has begun with Abraham, Isaac and Jacob, he will complete at the end of time.

Through God Israel's history is sanctified history; through God's election Israel is the holy nation; through God's wonder-ful guidance out of an Israel now so unsanctified there will one day appear the truly sanctified Israel even though, as punishment for its disobedience, it will only come after the Gentiles. How is this to happen?

[17]But if some of the branches were broken off, and you, a wild olive shoot, were grafted in their place to share the richness of the olive tree, [18]do not boast over the branches. If you do boast, remember it is not you that support the root, but the root that supports you. [19]You will say, "Branches were broken off so that I might be grafted in." [20]That is true. They were broken off because of their unbelief, but you stand fast only through faith. So do not become proud, but stand in awe. [21]For if God did not spare the natural branches, neither will he spare you. [22]Note then the kindness and severity of God: severity toward those who have fallen, but God's kindness to you,

provided you continue in his kindness; otherwise you too will be cut off. ²³And even the others, if they do not persist in their unbelief, will be grafted in, for God has the power to graft them in again. ²⁴For if you have been cut off from what is by nature a wild olive tree, and grafted, contrary to nature, into a cultivated olive tree, how much more will these natural branches be grafted back into their own olive tree.

Israel's fall and rejection is the means in the hand of God for sending salvation to the Gentiles. Israel is first of all "cut out". An alien has been ingrafted on the tree of Abraham. The Gentiles nourish themselves on the rich root of the patriarchal promise. Is it any praise to the Gentiles that God has given them the salvation which the Jews rejected? It is truly not due to their merit. On the other hand, they could certainly lose what has been granted to them in this way. We cannot give ourselves faith, yet we are responsible if we lose it and fall into unbelief. That would indeed be our fault. Thus it is always right to look at both sides: To remember gratefully the grace of God, to which alone we owe our salvation; and to remind ourselves in solemn earnestness of God's severity, which rejects him who is unfaithful.

The missionary to the Gentiles from the Jewish people has a special word to say to his Gentile Christians. They are now the ones who are favoured; certainly, their advantage does not derive from themselves, yet they are allowed to share as a gift in the blessing that was promised to Abraham. They have come into Abraham's inheritance. To whom do they owe this? They owe it to Israel's guilt and God's grace, but truly not to themselves. It is really entering into a legacy from which no one can benefit less than the heir. From his point of view there is absolutely no reason for it to turn out like that. Conversely one has, however, seriously to reckon with the possibility that those who by nature belong to the family of Abraham will also receive his inheritance. They also will receive it as soon as they give up their resistance and believe. The Gentile who is now a believer has therefore no reason whatever to exalt himself above the Jew. He ought to take to himself a warning example and allow himself to be told by him that faith is not capital from which one can draw interest. We remember here the words that are written in another letter: "Let anyone who thinks that he stands take heed lest he fall" (1 Cor. 10: 12).

The Wisdom of God Leads All Mankind to the Goal (11: 25-36)

²⁵Lest you be wise in your own conceits, I want you to understand this mystery, brethren: a hardening has come upon part of Israel, until the full number of the Gentiles come in, ²⁶and so all Israel will be saved; as it is written,

"The Deliverer will come from Zion,
he will banish ungodliness from Jacob";
²⁷"and this will be my covenant with them
when I take away their sins."

²⁸As regards the gospel they are enemies of God, for your sake; but as regards election they are beloved for the sake of their forefathers. ²⁹For the gifts and the call of God are irrevocable. ³⁰Just as you were once disobedient to God but now have received mercy because of their disobedience, ³¹so they have now been disobedient in order that by the mercy shown to you they also may receive mercy. ³²For God has consigned all men to disobedience, that he may have mercy upon all.

³³O the depth of the riches and wisdom and knowledge of God! How unsearchable are his judgments and how inscrutable his ways!

³⁴"For who has known the mind of the Lord,
or who has been his counsellor?"
³⁵"Or who has given a gift to him
that he might be repaid?"
³⁶For from him and through him and to him are all things. To him be glory forever. Amen.

Hitherto the apostle has only weighed the possibility that Israel's obstinacy might, after all, not be final. Now the full assurance breaks through. He, the apostle to the Gentiles, may and must reveal to the Romans a divine mystery entrusted to him, so that he may finally destroy all Gentile-Christian presumption. The entire letter, of course, offers sufficient guarantee that on the other side the Jewish or Jewish-Christian self-assertion does also not spring up again. This aspect of the educational task has been thoroughly taken care of, so that Paul, without having henceforth to fear any misunderstanding, can say: they who are now still God's enemies, as enemies of the Gospel and of the Church of Jesus, are, however, the loved ones of God in virtue of the election and for the sake of the inheritance of the forefathers.

Even the temporary unbelief of the Jews is included in God's plan of salvation. The Jews are not the expelled but the reinstated. In the last resort both Jews and Gentiles are equal before God. Both have at the beginning said No to God, and then by God's mercy faith is nevertheless bestowed upon them. The Jews must wait until all this has happened to the Gentiles —and this having to wait is the punishment for their disobedience. But at last their turn comes, too. God wants to show unmistakably through his guiding of history: as for mankind— Jews and Gentiles—disobedience; as for God's action—towards Jews and Gentiles—mercy. All come to salvation as those who were at first rejected; but they do come to salvation.

Paul himself is overwhelmed by the view of the history of redemption granted him here. His faltering words offer us a hint of something of the mystery of such a revelation which has come upon him—perhaps while writing the letter. The way from the ninth to the eleventh chapter along which he leads the reader is the way that God Himself has led him in the knowledge of his decree, from the anxious question: is therefore Israel, which rejects the Lord, itself rejected? to the view of the salvation of all at the end of the eleventh chapter. But this way is different from our ways. When we have gone a certain way, then it lies behind us and we may forget it because of the goal. We ought not to understand the apostle thus. This way must be trodden continually in order to reach the goal. The eleventh chapter is not true without the ninth, just as the message of the divine mercy is not true without that of the judgment.

Does Paul teach here what has continually emerged in some form in the Church as the doctrine of "universal salvation" but which has been rejected again and again as a heresy? How else is one to understand this "that he may have mercy upon all"? Therefore there is no "being lost", no hell, no condemnation; thus everything, though perhaps in a long roundabout way, turns out well for everyone after all whether they have believed or not, whether they have striven or not? Therefore it is all the same in the end after all—namely, everyone will be saved?

Paul is as far removed from this final conclusion as he is from the doctrine of the double decree. He does not state the one any more than the other. But as closely as he approaches the one by what he says, so does he also come close to the other. While reading the magnificently comforting words of the eleventh chapter, we ought not to forget the terribly serious words of the ninth chapter. There is here no simple balance sheet, no adding up with a straightforward result below the final line. The whole letter to the Romans is like a single sentence whose beginning is not cancelled out by the end but where beginning and end belong inseparably and irretrievably together. Whoever wanted to say: I go by the end where it is stated that God has mercy on all; whatever may have been said before, this, at all events, is the result and decides the issue—would necessarily have to become frivolous. Life then would have lost its tension and faith its decisiveness. On the other hand whoever wanted to make a stand at the ninth chapter with its hard words on the potter and the clay, the vessels of wrath beside the vessels of honour and the declarations about hardness, would have to sink into melancholy or learn to curse God. In each case one forgets that it is God Himself who wants to speak to us. It is not a question of a Christian theory of history, whether a two-dimensional or one-dimensional, but a question of God revealing Himself to us in his gravity and in his mercy, threatening our frivolity with judgment, inviting with the cry of the All-Merciful in face of our despair.

The apostle does not take us up into a look-out tower with a view of the world from which we can now see how everything will turn out; but the view which he offers us must also serve immediately again as the insight which shows us our absolutely serious responsibility. Thus the letter to the Romans does not close with this climax but descends again "below" into our everyday life; for what it is concerned with is that the will of God may come to pass. Therefore the "ethical" chapters 12-15 now follow.

Part Three

THE LIFE OF THE CHRISTIAN (12: 1—16: 16)

THE NEW RULE (12: 1-2)

[1]I appeal to you therefore, brethren, by the mercies of God, to present your bodies as a living sacrifice, holy and acceptable to God, which is your spiritual worship. [2]Do not be conformed to this world but be transformed by the renewal of your mind, that you may prove what is the will of God, what is good and acceptable and perfect.

THE letter hitherto has dealt with the change that has taken place in men's lives through God's saving act. Of course, not as if man were in this only a will-less vessel or dead material for the divine action, but always in such a way that God's acting sets the will of man in motion, giving it a new direction and strength. Yet only the most general outlines of this new "walking" have been sketched in the sixth and eighth chapters. Of this one must speak more thoroughly, giving instruction in every detail so that the community may understand that Jesus Christ in becoming ours became precisely the Lord of our everyday life, so that our Christian position must demonstrate itself in the particular details of practical life. To this task the apostle now addresses himself, after having taken us to the loftiest height and the lowest depth of the divine ruling of salvation.

But what follows now must not on any account be looked upon as a mere postscript which does not carry the same weight as what preceded it. Quite the contrary. One may say in a certain sense that the entire letter has been directed at this practical goal. Paul does not forget for a moment that God claims, not only the thinking, but also the will and action of men. Just as little could one say that something new is beginning now—after the "dogmatics", the "ethics". Even now this is not an independent morality. But as the fruit grows from the sap of the tree, so this instruction for the true Christian life grows out of what has been previously told us about God's merciful dealings with us. Therefore Paul appeals "by the mercies of God". In this way everything that has been said about God's giving and helping grace can be summed up. Paul neither teaches nor gives an order; he only appeals, inasmuch as everyone who stands in faith and has come to know the mercy of God realizes what is now at stake in the practical life. He only needs to be reminded of it.

To this also corresponds the content of the first appeal: Present yourselves as a sacrifice. Our sacrifice corresponds to Christ's Sacrifice, the self-surrender of the saved to the self-surrender of the Saviour. For we have been baptized into his death and are crucified with him. Therefore we must also lead a sacrificial life. The organ of action, the body, must now become an organ and instrument of God. For this service it must continually be consecrated anew so that it may become fit for the working of what is holy. And this ever new self-surrender to service, this daily sacrifice of ourself, in which our self-will is destroyed so that God may totally and solely be entitled to the possession of our life, is the reasonable, the appropriate sacrifice. This altar and this sacrificial gift are the necessary practical consequence of the Cross of Christ.

If we belong to God we no longer belong to the world. The Christian faith does not indeed take men out of the world—it rather places them even more in its midst—but it looses them from their attachment to the world. The law of the world, the way of the world, can no longer be theirs after they have become God's. The surrender to God is simultaneously a break with the old ways of the world. One cannot please the world and God at the same time. One "cannot serve God and Mammon" (Matt. 6: 24). The entire life, therefore, must be reconstructed according to a new building plan. The Christian man must now adopt the architectural style of God and do away with the style of the world. It will still require hard work until this reconstruction has been completed in every single detail! But the important thing is that one shall know God's building plan in general. Thus the renewal must commence at the centre, with the knowledge of the divine will—whereby God's will is to be understood now quite concretely as that which God wants from me now, to-day and here.

Seeking to understand God's will daily, hourly—that is the first thing with which the reconstruction must begin, wherein the self-sacrifice must manifest itself. It is indeed a matter of reconstruction or rather transformation. Little as Paul trusts the unredeemed man standing under the Law, he nevertheless expects much from him who is now "in Christ", and whom he only needs to remind of the mercy of God. He expects him to be able to "transform himself", or, as one says to-day, "to change his mode of life" completely.

Conversely we see from this appeal that we must not think of what has happened and is happening to us through Christ as something that is automatically and mechanically effective. What Jesus Christ has done for us and what the Holy Spirit is doing to us must be received and operate by an inward act of man. Everything is God's work, yet we must ourselves believe, ourselves repent, return and change our ways. God does not treat the self of man as an object, like a carpenter planing his board—but he claims it. We must think, learn, reflect, will and feel entirely anew. By this sign everything that follows will have to be understood.

THE BODY AND ITS MEMBERS (12: 3-8)

³For by the grace given to me I bid every one among you not to think of himself more highly than he ought to think, but to think with sober judgment, each according to the measure of faith which God has assigned him. ⁴For as in one body we have many members, and all the members do not have the same function, ⁵so we, though many, are one body in Christ, and individually members one of another. ⁶Having gifts that differ according to the grace given to us, let us use them: if prophecy, in proportion to our faith: ⁷if service, in our serving; he who teaches, in his teaching: ⁸he who exhorts, in his exhortation; he who contributes, in liberality; he who gives aid, with zeal; he who does acts of mercy, with cheerfulness.

The first thing that Paul calls to mind in his appeal is: do not aim too high! Even the new life, even God's gift of the Spirit can lead a man into temptation; the danger of a wild enthusiasm is present. The apostle asserts two things against it. First, faith also has a standard. That which faith embraces is the same for all men, the one, entire Jesus Christ and his salvation. To that extent all his believers are equal. But not all have this faith in the same degree. There are beginners and there are those who are "perfect", there are those who are weak and others who are strong. No one ought to overestimate his measure of faith, but everyone ought to know what he may expect of himself according to his position of faith.

No one has the full measure, therefore all must perfect themselves. That is the second thing: everyone with his strength of faith is a serving member of the whole body of the community. The gift of the Spirit differs not only according to its strength but also according to its kind. Yet this variety means that one must come to the aid of the other. Everybody has something and there is something lacking in everyone. Thus an exchange takes place. But for this it is necessary that everyone serves with his own gift and that no one assumes he can and may do everything that others can and may do. Each one has also a place in the Community of Christ, and ought to fill it, but he ought not to be everywhere and want to take part in everything. What is true of the gift is true of the task, the service. Here, too, there is a proper order, but this proper order is derived not from outside as a compulsion but from within, out of the diversity of the gifts of the Holy Spirit.

In speaking of the one body, Paul speaks of the "Church" without using the word. For what Paul denotes by the word ecclesia, which is normally translated as Church, is just this: the fellowship of believers, the people of Christ in their unity. Their unity is Christ, their diversity the different kinds of believers with their gifts and services. The unity of the Community demands exactly the recognition of this difference and the observance of the frontiers that result from it. Each one is to do what God has allotted to him through his specific talent as a particular task. But just as Paul will not tolerate a confusion originating in spiritual self-overestimation, so his instructions are also not to be understood as models. This is not concerned with a bureaucratic demarcation of the spheres of duty and responsibility. The idea of the "offices" for instance which is introduced here, is not to be transferred from the realm of the legal order to that of the free order of the Spirit. It concerns "services"—this is the word which since Luther has been often translated by "office"—as they result in the form of tasks from the various gifts of the Spirit; but not "offices", an idea taken from the political sphere. It rests on the divine gift, not on a canonical decree, that everyone is (so to speak) being allocated his sphere of operation. Nothing lies further from the apostle's thought than a canonical regimentation. His instruction runs: notice what God gives you, then you will also know the task he sets you.

Therefore he is also not concerned about completeness of detail. In other passages, i.e., 1 Cor. 12: 7ff., quite different gifts and services are enumerated. The Community has and requires a great variety of services, as the body needs a great variety of organs and functions. There is, for instance, the gift of prophecy, the gift of understanding God's directions for the present time with special clearness. Or the gifts of serving the needy, of looking after the poor; the systematic and constant dealing with the destitute and their particular need also demands a special inward preparation. The same is true of teaching. In this case we are, of course, nowhere clearly told what Paul understands by teaching; possibly a kind of biblical instruction. The examples which follow clearly demonstrate how little Paul is thinking in terms of permanent offices. To practise exhortation, liberality and mercy—these are the things that are binding for every member of the Community. Here the only valid rule is: whatever you do, do it in the way it demands, neither perfunctorily nor flippantly but with a holy seriousness. Even the overseers are not simply "officials", but, like all the rest, they are those whom a special gift of the Spirit enables to lead in a particular service—whether a specific kind of appointment was then added to it or not. Thus there is specially urged upon them not an authoritative, ponderous behaviour but a serene disposition.

THE NEW ATTITUDE (12 : 9-21)

⁹Let love be genuine; hate what is evil, hold fast to what is good; ¹⁰love one another with brotherly affection; outdo one another in showing honour. ¹¹Never flag in zeal, be aglow with the Spirit, serve the Lord. ¹²Rejoice in your hope, be patient in tribulation, be constant in prayer. ¹³Contribute to the needs of the saints, practise hospitality.

¹⁴Bless those who persecute you; bless and do not curse them. ¹⁵Rejoice with those who rejoice, weep with those who weep. ¹⁶Live in harmony with one another; do not be haughty, but associate with the lowly; never be conceited. ¹⁷Repay no one evil for evil, but take thought for what is noble in the sight of all. ¹⁸If possible, so far as it depends upon you, live peaceably with all. ¹⁹Beloved, never avenge yourselves, but leave it to the wrath of God; for it is written, "Vengeance is mine, I will repay, says the Lord." ²⁰No, "if your enemy is hungry, feed him; if he is thirsty, give him drink; for by so doing you will heap burning coals upon his head." ²¹Do not be overcome by evil, but overcome evil with good.

As the new relationship to God can be summed up in the one word faith, so the new relationship to men can be summarized in the one word love. Since through faith the door becomes unlocked towards God, the one towards men is also opened.

This is known to everyone in the Community. Hidden faith becomes manifest in love. For that very reason it is exposed to hypocrisy. Precisely because the genuineness of the life of faith must prove itself in love, the danger of an artificial, fabricated love is never far away. Like faith, love must also spring forth continually fresh from the fountain of God; else it is insipid and unreal. But genuineness is sincere affection; for the genuine is that which is at one with a person. The person in his oneness is called the heart in the Bible. From that everything else follows, and it has been said so simply by the apostle that it requires no special exposition. "What genuine love does and does not do"—that might be the title of this section. It is worth while, however, to stress a few things in particular.

Love itself is quite personal; yet if it is not to degenerate into sentimentality or partiality it must include a strict objectivity: hatred against evil, faithful adherence to what is good. Love goes together with humility; thus it belongs to its nature to be more concerned about the praise of the other than of oneself. It is the living-in-another, therefore it is taking an interest in and giving a share to the other. In this way the law of action does not derive from the behaviour of the other but from the attitude of God; moreover it understands the other and wants to be his companion in everything, in joy and sorrow.

It tries to preserve fellowship through everything; thus every form of retaliation is contrary to it. If there must be judgment and punishment, that is a matter for God. Thus the Old Testament already knew that good-will and beneficence do not cease even towards the enemy. Therefore love bears with it the assurance that it is the superior power which can maintain itself in the world in face of evil and overcome it. To conquer malice with kindness—that is the superiority and freedom of love.

Among these thoughts concerning love are interspersed a few others that do not stand in a direct relation to them but which yet are part of the picture of the new life, thoughts that refer not to the operation but to the source of love towards men. Love comes only from the renewed attitude towards God which is its origin. The connection with God is God's work in Jesus Christ. Yet this very same connection with God must also continually be sought again by man and restored anew. There is needed always that turning which the hymn-writer means when he says: "Let hearts revive!" One must rub the spiritual sleep out of one's eyes, one must stir up the fire of the divine love, one must continually offer oneself consciously to the service of the Lord as the servant who comes before his master and asks what he is to do; one must not allow oneself to be depressed by adverse circumstances—in short, it needs that secret life with God whose most positive expression is prayer. To live truly with one's neighbour: that is love. To live truly with God: that is prayer. These two things make up the whole of the Christian life.

But are there not also still other "duties" in the Christian life which are neither love nor prayer, the life in the world of ordinances, of which the most important is that of the State? The next chapter supplies the information on that point.

CHRISTIANS AND THE POLITICAL ORDER (13: 1-7)

[1]Let every person be subject to the governing authorities. For there is no authority except from God, and those that exist have been instituted by God. [2]Therefore he who resists the authorities resists what God has appointed, and those who resist will incur judgment. [3]For rulers are not a terror to good conduct, but to bad. Would you have no fear of him who

is in authority? Then do what is good, and you will receive his approval, ⁴for he is God's servant for your good. But if you do wrong, be afraid, for he does not bear the sword in vain; he is the servant of God to execute his wrath on the wrongdoer. ⁵Therefore one must be subject, not only to avoid God's wrath but also for the sake of conscience. ⁶For the same reason you also pay taxes, for the authorities are ministers of God, attending to this very thing. ⁷Pay all of them their dues, taxes to whom taxes are due, revenue to whom revenue is due, respect to whom respect is due, honour to whom honour is due.

Placed between the two powerful testimonies to love as the epitome of the Christian life, these explanations of the relationship of Christians to the "authorities" appear at first like a foreign body. For what has obedience to the State, which does not wield the sword in vain, and what has the paying of taxes and revenue, to do with love? Has Paul perhaps for a moment lost the thread, digressing here into a sphere that has nothing to do with the Christian life as such? The apostle knows full well what he is doing. If he is dealing with the Christian life, this burning question of how we stand in relation to the State cannot be avoided.

If the political order, with its impersonality and hard legalism, is something alien to the new life in Christ, the life in love, then the difficulty of finding a bridge between the two is so much the greater as it is the pagan, godless Roman Empire with which he is here dealing. It is the State which crucified the Lord Jesus and oppressed the Jewish people; the State which by force compels every nation to bestow religious honours upon the emperor; it is above all the State of the terrible Nero. What is the right attitude of the Community of Jesus Christ towards it, and what is to be thought of it from the point of view of faith in God's will revealed in Jesus Christ?

Without showing even the slightest vacillation Paul demands in the sharpest form of command, which otherwise is missing in his appeals, obedient submission to governmental authority —and that not merely external but inwardly conscientious: everyone—to be precise: every soul—must be subject to it. The apostle does not fail to give a reason for this command, yet this is also at first again something of a puzzle: all magisterial power is from God. It is perhaps not an accident that

Paul is using here the same word by which he elsewhere denotes supernatural angelic powers. He thus sees in the State an instrument of God. The Christian ought to obey not the State, not men, but God, even where God does not confront him in his own direct word of revelation but through his "servants". God's order and God's will stand behind the State; those who rule are his servants, even if they do not know it. Paul does not pose the necessity of the State, he does not inquire into the usefulness of the State. He looks at its work, recognizing in it the hand of God.

The magisterial powers are the custodians of public order and of a sure, even if rough, justice. It is the State which gives practical effect to the verdict of the judge and the command of the law. It is in the public relation of the State to the law that Paul discovers the trail of God. Through it the divine wrath intervenes over the injustice in the human reality behind the human instrument (however human it may be); the divine will for righteousness becomes visible. No form of State glorification, no defence or justification of the State is asserted here, but solely reverence before God, who also deals with men by means of this instrument and demands from them obedience.

Thus we are not at first concerned with so-called duties towards the State. Whoever lives as a disciple of Jesus, doing what is good and not what is evil, does not come into conflict with the State which is guarding the law. The duty of subordination is nothing but the acknowledgment of the divine servant and instrument. Where Jesus Christ and the Holy Spirit with his love are not yet effective, there the law is still valid, and there this rough external order of the law is also still applicable. Opposition to it would be opposition to God's operation of wrath. What really matters, therefore, is that this subordination shall not happen merely because of external reasons, because of punishment, but out of an obligation of conscience, since it does not concern the State as such or the servants, but the Lord Himself. The possessors of political power are instruments of the divine rule of wrath to which we ought to give place. That is the dignity, that is also the limit of the State.

Thus every member of the Community must also render

unto Caesar what is Caesar's (Matt. 22: 21). His taxes, his revenues, his social scale belong to his sphere; as the State itself, so its means are also to be acknowledged. It does not concern the acknowledgment of an abstract idea of the State, but the actual State and its real action. In this its real action it becomes the executor of the divine will—not of his will of salvation but his will of wrath; it is part of the order of this world that passes away, whose mode of operation is therefore quite different from that which belongs to the Christian Community as such and with which Christians as such, moreover, ought to have nothing to do (1 Cor. 6: 1-7). There are many questions we would like to ask the apostle here, questions that force themselves upon us from a two-thousand-years-old history of peaceful and hostile argument between the Christian Community and the State. The apostle does not give us an answer to them, since our historical situation, of course, is quite different from his. There can as yet be no question of a responsibility towards the State—responsibility for co-operation as well as for improvement or criticism—since the Christian Community had, of course, no possibility at all of influencing the State in any way. Hence on the basis of these brief references by the apostle one cannot arrive at a Christian political theory such as has become a necessity for us to-day.

Yet the remarkable fact remains that these explanations are interposed between two instructions concerning Christian love! Obviously, there exists for Paul a hidden relationship after all. I think it is not too difficult to find. Love is not a levelling; love meets everyone as the person he is and takes him seriously in his particular being. To confront the representatives of political power with the intention of giving them their due, is an outworking of love.

Neither Paul, nor Christians in their lives, are concerned with the abstract entity of the State, but with persons who have something definite to do, who occupy a definite position and expect something definite from them. To give them what is their due, to owe them no debt, is the command of love. Indeed, love itself is not abstract and theoretical, but it consists precisely—as we shall hear in the next section—in fulfilling the law by acknowledging everyone in the place in which God has put him and giving him that which he requires for the fulfilment of his special task of service. How can one love the official if one does not acknowledge his office and its dignity? Love does not presuppose justice, but love spontaneously fulfils the demands of justice. This will be dealt with in the next section.

LOVE AS THE FULFILMENT OF THE LAW (13: 8-10)

8Owe no one anything, except to love one another; for he who loves his neighbour has fulfilled the law. 9The commandments, "You shall not commit adultery, You shall not kill, You shall not steal, You shall not covet," and any other command-ment, are summed up in this sentence, "You shall love your neighbour as yourself." 10Love does no wrong to a neighbour; therefore love is the fulfilling of the law.

To owe no one anything—that is the principle of justice. "To everyone his own." With that Paul concludes his remarks regarding the attitude of the Christian to the authorities. Yet this "owing no one anything" is not separate and in-dependent, but is embedded in something still greater. Who-ever owes nothing to anyone parts from the other once he has done his duty.

Love is greater than justice; it does more than justice demands. The demand of justice ends with the individual; love alone is all-embracing because it does not keep its eye on "something" that one owes the other but on the other himself and myself. I owe myself to him and therefore I am never done with him. Once more we encounter the theme of the letter to the Romans: the Law. Once again the question is being answered from a new point of view. The Law, the content of the commandments, does not mean at all "this and that" as it must seem so long as one has to do only with the Law as such. The commandments always mean the one thing: Love. That which in the Law is expressed in isolated demands proves to be unique from the point of view of faith in Jesus Christ and the love revealed in him. So long as we stand "under the Law" we cannot perceive this hidden unity of all the commandments. It is part of legalism that the will of God must appear to it as a multiplicity of commandments. In actual fact it is one and indivisible; God wants nothing else except love because he himself is love. God's commandments, rightly understood, always declare one thing only: love your neighbour. There are individual examples as to what this love will mean in individual cases—just as the Lord in the Sermon on the Mount expounded the commandments as commandments of love. As God in Jesus Christ gives and wills himself entirely to us so we, too, ought to give ourselves entirely to our neighbour, entirely embrace him with our love. If we do that, then there is no further need of any law; then everything that the law demands has been done.

In the commandment of love the whole law is summed up; yet the commandment of love can be neither correctly understood nor rightly fulfilled as law. To fulfil it we must have love, of course, but we cannot bestow his love upon ourselves! It is the nature of love that it must "flow" freely, as Luther said. That which springs from one's own effort is certainly not love. Love is either present, because "it has been poured into our hearts through the Holy Spirit" after we have been united with God by faith in the reconciliation through Jesus Christ— or it is not present at all. But if it is present, then it fulfils all that the law demands. It is pure good-will towards the other, and therefore does only good to him and not evil. That this love is now present, so that one only needs to remember it, is the gift of God in Jesus Christ, the fruit of faith "which is working through love" (Gal. 5: 6).

WAITING FOR THE CONSUMMATION (13: 11-14)

[11]Besides this you know what hour it is, how it is full time now for you to wake from sleep. For salvation is nearer to us now than when we first believed; [12]the night is far gone, the day is at hand. Let us then cast off the works of darkness and put on the armour of light; [13]let us conduct ourselves becomingly as in the day, not in revelling and drunkenness, not in debauchery and licentiousness, not in quarrelling and jealousy. [14]But put on the Lord Jesus Christ, and make no provision for the flesh, to gratify its desires.

The remembrance of what God's mercy in Jesus Christ has done for us is one powerful impulse of the new life; the other, which is inseparably linked with it, is the sure expectation of

what he will do. Where faith in Christ looks at the future, it
turns into hope. Yet this future is not remote—something that
glimmers on the distant horizon of history. It is the future of the
Lord, and this future is already in process of happening.

With every hour we approach it more closely; already it
throws its light into the darkness of the present. Faith is indeed
nothing but living in the light of that which is to come. Therefore faith is living by day, not night-life. To believe is to be
watchful, and not to sleep—we are reminded of the many
parables of the Lord regarding watchfulness, the watchful servants and the watchful virgins, etc. The present of the Christians
is a waiting before the Lord. Therefore we ought no longer
to have anything to do with "night-life". We have become
people of the day. Darkness is seclusion from the light of God;
whoever stands in God's light can no longer have anything to
do with the works of darkness. The works of darkness are
everything which arises from forgetfulness of God, whatever
can thrive only where God's light does not penetrate. Whoever
wanted to participate in them would have to cut himself off
again from God and to step out of his light. But he who knows
God must renounce this whole world of darkness.

That, of course, can only happen if we continually place
ourselves in God's light, if we "put on the Lord Jesus Christ".
The whole Christian life is a putting off and a putting on—
the old man must be put off, the new man put on. It is not
true that in "conversion" or "rebirth" everything has happened as a once-for-all event. Even though the event of
baptism may signify such a clean break in that—as in missionary baptism—this putting off and putting on is taking place
for the very first time, yet the turning away from the old life
and the coming to Christ must be continually repeated.
Continually we must fight the fight of faith, continually "enter"
the death and resurrection of the Lord, continually put away
what does not belong to God and "take hold of eternal life"
(1 Tim. 6: 12).

Jesus Christ has set us on the new ground, but the sinful flesh
continually draws us away from him, thus making a new
turning to him necessary. The appeal, therefore, closes with a
particular warning not to cultivate the flesh in a manner that
makes it lascivious. The pastoral realism of the apostle enables

him to take especially seriously these very things that stand in closest proximity to the "night-life", for he knows what a favourable gate of entrance just this part of our nature offers to the power of evil. It begins with a little self-indulgence and immediately one lands once more in darkness. Therefore it is necessary to set up just on this side a signal that cannot be overlooked.

FREEDOM AND FELLOWSHIP (14: 1-12)

¹As for the man who is weak in faith, welcome him, but not for disputes over opinions. ²One believes he may eat anything, while the weak man eats only vegetables. ³Let not him who eats despise him who abstains, and let not him who abstains pass judgment on him who eats; for God has welcomed him. ⁴Who are you to pass judgment on the servant of another? It is before his own master that he stands or falls. And he will be upheld, for the Master is able to make him stand.

⁵One man esteems one day as better than another, while another man esteems all days alike. Let every one be fully convinced in his own mind. ⁶He who observes the day, observes it in honour of the Lord. He also who eats, eats in honour of the Lord, since he gives thanks to God; while he who abstains, abstains in honour of the Lord and gives thanks to God. ⁷None of us lives to himself, and none of us dies to himself. ⁸If we live, we live to the Lord, and if we die, we die to the Lord; so then, whether we live or whether we die, we are the Lord's. ⁹For to this end Christ died and lived again, that he might be Lord both of the dead and of the living.

¹⁰Why do you pass judgment on your brother? Or you, why do you despise your brother? For we shall all stand before the judgment seat of God; ¹¹for it is written,

"As I live, says the Lord, every knee shall bow to me,
    and every tongue shall give praise to God."
¹²So each of us shall give account of himself to God.

By using a further example from the life of the Community Paul makes clear what is meant by living with Christ. Manifestly a certain split has occurred in the Church at Rome between a group of nervous people who observed strict food regulations for religious reasons, and also certain holy days, and others who condemned such anxiety as a sign that their faith lacked freedom. The nervous ones we probably have to seek among the Jewish Christians, who were afraid of being given meat sacrificed to idols at the meat market and who did not like giving up the holy days of their people; on their part they considered the "libertarians" careless. Paul in principle sides with the libertarians; but in practice he protects the others from a certain arrogance on the part of the libertarians, though not without sharply reprimanding a certain Pharisaism among the others. This matter, unimportant in itself, is raised by him to the highest level because of its relation to the end. For it does, indeed, concern the end; it concerns freedom and obligation, earnestness of conscience and divine adoption. The apostle draws up two rules: Conscience must not be injured at any price—even if it is not an entirely free conscience. And the fellowship must not for the sake of such differences be dissolved or endangered. Freedom in Christ—certainly; but also mutual respect in Christ. On no account must they question each other's sincerity or despise one another.

With this question Paul makes it clear that for the Christian there is no longer any tie except to the Lord Himself. Subject directly to the king alone! If both parties are sure that they only want to do the will of the Lord, then they can have a mutual approval. The Lord after all has servants of differing types in his service; it is not our business to decide who really does his will. That Paul does not want thereby to eliminate every kind of possibility of criticizing the attitude of a member of the Community is clear from what we previously heard. Where the question concerns God's law there is no uncertainty, for love fulfils the law. Where no clear norm is evident, however, one must leave the question open and point everyone to the Lord Himself. For he himself is the norm; as Christians we are subject to no law but only to him who, however, has made known his will to us in the law, at least in certain directions.

The Christian life, life in the Community, means living as one who belongs to Christ, no longer having one's own will. From the very beginning we belong to God as his creatures. But because this first, original connection and tie has been destroyed by our sin, God has fastened it again and at the same time more closely in Jesus Christ. We have been "bought with a price" (1 Cor. 6: 20); it cost nothing less than the life of the Lord

for us to become again the property of God. But now we are
that through faith, in life and in death. We are united with him
for all eternity—that is his gift of salvation; and bound to him
—that is our sacred task. The whole life and death of our Lord
is Messianic, its only meaning is the setting up of the lordship
of God. Yet this thought of bondage to Christ receives its full
weight only in reference to judgment. It gets its seriousness
from the fact that all our activity and inactivity extend to that
point and have in it their standard of value; only in view of
the judgment does the word "responsibility" receive its full
meaning. And yet Paul does not say this to frighten. He
confidently dares to say to both sides, and even to the "weak":
the Lord helps you through so that you will not fall. There is,
of course, only one real kind of falling: to fall away from the
Lord Himself. Whoever abides in the Lord, the Lord will also
stand by him—in spite of weakness and error.

THE CONSCIENCE OF THE OTHER PERSON (14: 13—15: 4)

[13]Then let us no more pass judgment on one another, but
rather decide never to put a stumbling-block or hindrance in
the way of a brother. [14]I know and am persuaded in the Lord
Jesus that nothing is unclean in itself; but it is unclean for any
one who thinks it unclean. [15]If your brother is being injured by
what you eat, you are no longer walking in love. Do not
let what you eat cause the ruin of one for whom Christ died.
[16]So do not let what is good to you be spoken of as evil. [17]For
the kingdom of God does not mean food and drink but righteousness and peace and joy in the Holy Spirit; [18]he who
thus serves Christ is acceptable to God and approved by men.
[19]Let us then pursue what makes for peace and for mutual
upbuilding. [20]Do not, for the sake of food, destroy the work
of God. Everything is indeed clean, but it is wrong for anyone
to make others fall by what he eats; [21]it is right not to eat
meat or drink wine or do anything that makes your brother
stumble. [22]The faith that you have, keep between yourself
and God; happy is he who has no reason to judge himself
for what he approves. [23]But he who has doubts is condemned, if
he eats, because he does not act from faith; for whatever does
not proceed from faith is sin.
15. [1]We who are strong ought to bear with the failings of
the weak, and not to please ourselves; [2]let each of us please his
neighbour for his good, to edify him. [3]For Christ did not please

himself; but, as it is written, "The reproaches of those who reproached thee fell on me." [4]For whatever was written in former days was written for our instruction, that by steadfastness and by the encouragement of the scriptures we might have hope.

Mutual criticism is not the only danger in the fellowship; we can also harm each other inwardly by our actions, not only by our talking and the way in which we think of one another. Harm is done by actions of ours which in themselves are the right thing. There is a devout carelessness in doing what one has recognized as right for oneself but which can ruin one's neighbour. Faith alone is not a sufficient basis for life in the fellowship. What God permits to me and what is therefore the right thing for me need not for that reason be at all the right thing for others. One must, out of love, show an additional consideration for others. A straightforward zealous faith, a proud and bold faith can, where it is not guided by tender consideration for what is beneficial for the other, lead to his ruin. What was more likely than that the fighter against all legalism should in some way brand the legalistic anxiety of the "weak" as being such, and advance with warlike ruthlessness against them or at least pass them by! But Paul is not only a preacher but also a pastor. He is not merely an ambassador but also a founder of Christian communities. He has not just one great word, faith, but two, faith and love. Faith establishes the new life but love determines it. And love demands consideration for the weak. Where it is a question of the outworking of faith, there is no abstract principle but only a demand: to do no evil to the other but only good.

Paul leaves us in no doubt that for him the scruples of the nervous do not exist. "All is yours." To him who is pure everything is pure. But only—to the pure! He who has found full freedom in Jesus Christ no longer requires any legal crutches; yet the other still needs them until he himself acquires the perfect knowledge. If one takes them from him, then one makes him do something by example, for which he does not yet possess the inner freedom, for which he can therefore inwardly in fact not be fully responsible. Then one injures him; indeed, one can even ruin him. This price must not be paid for the demonstration of my freedom of faith. Faith bestows an inner freedom but no external one. Faith does not tell me what I may do; that is what love says to me. Faith tells me how matters stand between God and me, but not how things are between me and my neighbour. My attitude to my neighbour is not determined by my freedom of faith but according to the rule of love, which demands that I do nothing which harms my neighbour, even though I had a thousand times the right to do such an action according to my faith!

Paul now brings up his heaviest artillery: Do you want to ruin him for whom Christ has died? Love means watching over one another so that the Kingdom of God, which is the concern of the Christian life, is "built up". God's Kingdom is not determined by anything external; the what of the action never matters there, but only the why. The Kingdom of God exists where God reigns in the heart, where the innermost part of man is reconciled with God. It does not require for its external demonstration any special mark of freedom. It is the inmost freedom that makes possible the free obligation to what is necessary for others.

The pastor knows no devout carelessness. The conscience of the other is holy to him. For what is to become of his faith if he—led astray by the example of the strong—does what is against his conscience? Paul has, and teaches, respect for the conscience of the other—even though he may be wrong! For faith must take root and grow in the conscience. If the conscience is destroyed, then faith also is done for. Indeed, in the end Paul looks upon conscience and faith as being so closely allied that for a moment he classes them as one. For the sentence: "What does not proceed from faith is sin" must not be interpreted in the sense of the old dogmaticians—in this context it is not saying that all that is good is derived from faith; that every action, therefore, not derived from faith is sin, true as this statement is in itself—but it must be understood from the context: "Everything not done with a good conscience is sin from the very start." It is better for someone to do what is in itself wrong but do it with a good conscience than to do with a bad conscience what in itself may be better.

The devout carelessness or pious want of consideration stands in contrast to the action of the Lord Himself. He has taken the form of a servant (Phil. 2: 7), he humbled himself, he not only took upon himself the weakness but also the sins of others, he let himself and his freedom become nothing for the sake of others. His entire life was consideration in the deepest sense, living for others, doing that which is of service to others. In other words: Christ shows us that there are no pious rights. The "strong" by themselves had a right to eat meat, to drink wine, etc.; but this right fades before love. Christ never acted according to rights but always from love, i.e., from consideration towards others. In this way we should read the Bible. Everywhere it deals with this way of the Cross, with this renunciation of one's own right, with the men of God who had to go this lowly way and sacrifice their lives. As they bore the heaviest burden, so we wish to do it, too. A view of the whole Bible shows us that the way downward is the right way, the way which leads to the glory of the resurrection.

UNITY IN DIVERSITY (15: 5-13)

⁵May the God of steadfastness and encouragement grant you to live in such harmony with one another, in accord with Christ Jesus, ⁶that together you may with one voice glorify the God and Father of our Lord Jesus Christ.

⁷Welcome one another, therefore, as Christ has welcomed you for the glory of God. ⁸For I tell you that Christ became a servant to the circumcised to show God's truthfulness, in order to confirm the promises given to the patriarchs, ⁹and in order that the Gentiles might glorify God for his mercy. As it is written,

"Therefore I will praise thee among the Gentiles,
and sing to thy name";
¹⁰and again it is said,
"Rejoice, O Gentiles, with his people";
¹¹and again,
"Praise the Lord, all Gentiles,
and let all the peoples praise him";
¹²and further Isaiah says,
"The root of Jesse shall come,
he who rises *to* rule the Gentiles;
in him shall the Gentiles hope."

¹³May the God of hope fill you with all joy and peace in believing, so that by the power of the Holy Spirit you may abound in hope.

Although there are differences in the Christian Community which cannot now be eliminated, there ought not, however, to be any division. As in almost all the letters of Paul, there is here too an urgent appeal for unity. There is thus a unity above the oppositions, above our various religious conceptions and points of view: the unity in Jesus Christ Himself. No difference must prevent everyone from thanking God in common for the gift which they have received in Jesus Christ. In the common praise of God the Community is able continually to find the threatened unity; yet in the common praise of God it must also continually show itself as a unity. If it were no longer able to do this, if one could no longer praise and thank God in common, then the differences would indeed have ended in a fatal division.

But there is still another reason for unity: the welcoming of one another in diversity. This welcoming of the other in his otherness has been shown to us by Christ. He, the Holy One, has welcomed us, the sinners. This welcoming of one another is love—the true love, the love of Christ. Natural love takes only to the same kind, it accepts those who are sympathetic and pleasant to oneself. Christ's example demonstrates the opposite: he received those who nailed him to the Cross. He welcomed those who resisted him. The fact that the whole Community and all faith is based upon this is no longer the question here; that is simply presupposed after everything that has been said. So much the more may we remember it as the great example of welcome and live after the manner that Christ has made a norm for us. To welcome one another in all diversity, yes, even in every kind of opposition: that is the essence of love which guarantees the unity of the Community, the unity of love in which God is honoured and also the unity which is necessary for the common praise of God.

Jesus welcomed them both, the Jews and the Gentiles. He first became a servant of the circumcised, of Judaism. In their synagogues he interpreted the Law; he kept their precepts; his immediate service was directed chiefly and almost exclusively towards his people. Yet it took place in a work of salvation for humanity in which God's promises for all nations reach their fulfilment. Salvation is, as the Gospel of St. John says, from the Jews, but it is for the entire world. The opposition between

Jews and Gentiles is overcome in Christ; he himself has abolished it, thereby fulfilling the hope of the patriarchs and the predictions of the prophets. As Christ has put an end to this opposition, so every opposition in the Community ought also to disappear even though the differences continue. In the mutual welcoming of one another they lose their divisive power. In view of God's great goal for the nations they must become harmless. Thus there are three great gifts necessary in the Community in order that the Community may really become the Fellowship: faith which looks to the work of Christ as the basis of salvation; hope, which gazes towards the goal of consummation that shines in the work of Christ; and love, wherein the welcoming of one another takes place as the fruit of having been received by Christ. These are the fruits of the Holy Spirit: joy at the gift of Christ, peace with one another in the fellowship, and the hope of consummation.

THE WORLD-WIDE TASK AND FELLOWSHIP (15: 14-33)

[14]I myself am satisfied about you, my brethren, that you yourselves are full of goodness, filled with all knowledge, and able to instruct one another. [15]But on some points I have written to you very boldly by way of reminder, because of the grace given me by God [16]to be a minister of Christ Jesus to the Gentiles in the priestly service of the gospel of God, so that the offering of the Gentiles may be acceptable, sanctified by the Holy Spirit. [17]In Christ Jesus, then, I have reason to be proud of my work for God. [18]For I will not venture to speak of anything except what Christ has wrought through me to win obedience from the Gentiles, by word and deed, [19]by the power of signs and wonders, by the power of the Holy Spirit, so that from Jerusalem and as far round as Illyricum I have fully preached the gospel of Christ.

In approaching the end of the letter, the apostle again remembers his personal relation to the Community of Rome as he did at the beginning.

It sounds almost like an apology: forgive me for writing to you all this in such detail; actually, of course, you know all this already yourselves. For he is dealing not with beginners but with a proved Community, with reliable Christians whose fruits of the Spirit—as he mentioned at the beginning—are not hidden but well-known. They form a Community in which everything belonging to a true Christian Community is to be found. The audacity nevertheless of writing such a letter derives from his special missionary task, from the particular sacred service which has been entrusted to him: to bring Christ to the Gentiles, and thereby to bring the Gentiles to God. Once more it becomes evident that the proclamation of the Gospel does not consist of shouting an impersonal message into the world, as it were unconcerned about him who receives it, but that proclamation is at the same time a pastoral ministry, a priestly service for the souls of those to whom the message is brought, so that they become not merely recipients of the priestly sacrifice of Christ but a holy sacrifice themselves, sanctified by the Holy Spirit.

Nowhere is it merely concerned with a message but everywhere with an event. Paul thus never writes only as a theologian, as someone who has a certain knowledge about things, but as a missionary, a man who has experienced something of the power of the message that has been entrusted to him. What he says he says on the basis of such experience; he says nothing which has not been proved by experience. This experience, however, is nothing "subjective" but on the contrary something quite "objective": the effect of Christ throughout the entire world. The actual effect on which it depends is obedience. Indeed what he is concerned with, as he said at the beginning of the letter, is to preach so as to create obedience to Christ.

He himself, the apostle, is only an instrument in this matter; he cannot create obedience; this only Jesus Himself can do and does. But the means he employs for it are not unknown to the apostle. In the first place the Word; but to the Word must be immediately joined the deed. The Holy Spirit is also not so invisible as many assert: he appears in peculiar forms, in extraordinary results that correspond to the extraordinary cause. In this sense it is not always correct to stress only: the Word alone does it. No, the Holy Spirit alone does it, but he brings about the Word and the work, signs and wonders, too, which must all help together towards the awakening of faith and the producing of obedience to Christ. As such a sign the tremendous radius of operation of the Pauline mission may also be seen. He evangelized from Jerusalem as far as

Illyricum, and he did this not just superficially but "finished it entirely". This is the Paul on whom God bestowed this power of the Spirit, he who dared to claim the attention of the Roman Community for so long by such a detailed letter and such direct orders.

20Thus making it my ambition to preach the gospel, not where Christ has already been named, lest I build on another man's foundation, 21but as it is written,
"They shall see who have never been told of him,
and they shall understand who have never heard of him."
22This is the reason why I have so often been hindered from coming to you. 23But now, since I no longer have any room for work in these regions, and since I have longed for many years to come to you, 24I hope to see you in passing as I go to Spain, and to be sped on my journey there by you, once I have enjoyed your company for a little. 25At present, however, I am going to Jerusalem with aid for the saints. 26For Macedonia and Achaia have been pleased to make some contribution for the poor among the saints at Jerusalem; 27they were pleased to do it, and indeed they are in debt to them, for if the Gentiles have come to share in their spiritual blessings, they ought also to be of service to them in material blessings. 28When therefore I have completed this, and have delivered to them what has been raised, I shall go on by way of you to Spain; 29and I know that when I come to you I shall come in the fulness of the blessing of Christ.

30I appeal to you, brethren, by our Lord Jesus Christ and by the love of the Spirit, to strive together with me in your prayers to God on my behalf, 31that I may be delivered from the unbelievers in Judea, and that my service for Jerusalem may be acceptable to the saints, 32so that by God's will I may come to you with joy and be refreshed in your company. 33The God of peace be with you all. Amen.

Paul now lets the Roman Community look a little into his missionary strategy. That he does not want to build on an alien foundation and that he now considers his work in the East as finished has one and the same reason. He has a special task of world mission. Others may and must continue to build on the foundation that he has laid (cp. 1 Cor. 3: 6ff.); he himself has another order. There certainly was "in those regions"—i.e. in the entire East—still "room" enough, but not for him. What the signal for the apostle was that the time had come for him to move on, we do not exactly know. He did, of course, remain for quite a long time at several places without a break (cp. Acts 18: 11; 19: 10). It may be assumed that for him there were less definite principles for it than the special guidance of the Spirit (cp. Acts 16: 6, 7). But this basic principle remained unaltered for him: not to continue to work on soil already ploughed.

Herein he looks for his honour; it is obviously something which is connected with his particular commission. Because he is the missionary to the whole world, he does not consider what was quite in order for others (1 Cor. 3: 8): to continue to build on that which another had begun. All the same he wants to make an exception this time in so far as he wishes, on his passing through to Spain, at least to visit the community at Rome and, as it were, be provided with a spiritual *viaticum*. Indeed, he hopes that some from the Roman Community will accompany him as helpers. We see from these reports that for Paul strategic planning and guidance by the Holy Spirit were not at all in opposition.

Meantime the Spirit has led him in the opposite direction, towards Jerusalem. to which he intends to take the collection that was previously agreed upon at the "council of the apostles" (Gal. 2: 10) and which had since been keenly urged by Paul. These collections meant far more to him than merely a material action of relief for the poor of Jerusalem, of whom there were obviously many and in particularly urgent need. What he expounds in the second letter to the Corinthians (chapter 8-9) in great detail he compresses here into a short sentence. The collection is to be the return present of the Gentile congregations for the gift of the Gospel gone out from Jerusalem. It is thus an important sign of the unity of the two great groups in the Church: the Jews and the Gentiles. Therefore it matters to him to emphasize that the Greek Communities have by themselves decided on these collections.

The unity of the Church, with all its existing differences and even oppositions, thus receives expression in the act of helpful sacrificial love. On the other side, the apostle's request for the prayers of the Romans shows how much he cared that the original Church in Jerusalem and above all its leaders should also really see in this act of love a witness, even a proof, of the unity of the Communities. Obviously Paul is not quite sure of its favourable reception in Jerusalem by the leaders of the Christian Community there. That struggle of which the 15th chapter of the Acts of the Apostles and, much more clearly, the letter to the Galatians speak to us has not been fought to the end; the mistrust against the bold apostle of the Gentiles who declared the Mosaic law as not binding for the Gentiles has still not quite vanished. Paul as the youngest apostle and former persecutor of the Christian Community must still continue to fight for trust. That he was always conscious of the danger which threatened him from the "disobedient" Jews was brought home to him by the persecutions to which the Jews in the diaspora had already exposed him. How much more must the Jews in Jerusalem hate him!

In the foreground of his thoughts, however, stands neither of these two things but the anticipated joy of his visit to Rome, of the mutual exchange which he will bring. The apostle knows indeed that when he comes he will come with the fulness of blessing. The dependence on God's grace does not take on here the morbid form that the apostle would be unable to say anything at all as to whether God might bless him with his grace in Rome; but in spite of this proudly-humble self-assertion of one who has to give, the apostle is not self-sufficient but gladly looks forward to a renewed receiving. This exchange, however, can begin already even when they are separated. As the apostle is now linked to the Romans through this letter, so they should and can be joined to him through their intercessions. They both, as it were, meet before God's throne. Intercession is therefore strongly emphasized in all the letters of Paul, since it is this which links and unites the Community at the deepest level. Yet from this intercession there also emerges as the conclusion of the letter what is for Paul of the greatest importance and what we so easily overlook, or at any rate underestimate: the Greetings.

THE PERSONAL FELLOWSHIP EXPRESSED IN
SALUTATIONS (16: 1-16)

[1]I commend to you our sister Phoebe, a deaconess of the

church at Cenchreae, ²that you may receive her in the Lord as befits the saints, and help her in whatever she may require from you, for she has been a helper of many and of myself as well.

³Greet Prisca and Aquila, my fellow workers in Christ Jesus, ⁴who risked their necks for my life, to whom not only I but also all the churches of the Gentiles give thanks; ⁵greet also the church in their house. Greet my beloved Epaenetus, who was the first convert in Asia for Christ. ⁶Greet Mary, who has worked hard among you. ⁷Greet Andronicus and Junias, my kinsmen and my fellow prisoners; they are men of note among the apostles, and they were in Christ before me. ⁸Greet Ampliatus, my beloved in the Lord. ⁹Greet Urbanus, our fellow worker in Christ, and my beloved Stachys. ¹⁰Greet Apelles, who is approved in Christ. Greet those who belong to the family of Aristobulus. ¹¹Greet my kinsman Herodion. Greet those in the Lord who belong to the family of Narcissus. ¹²Greet those workers in the Lord, Tryphaena and Tryphosa. Greet the beloved Persis, who has worked hard in the Lord. ¹³Greet Rufus, eminent in the Lord, also his mother and mine. ¹⁴Greet Asyncritus, Phlegon, Hermes, Patrobas, Hermas, and the brethren who are with them. ¹⁵Greet Philologus, Julia, Nereus and his sister, and Olympas, and all the saints who are with them. ¹⁶Greet one another with a holy kiss. All the churches of Christ greet you.

A dry list of names—so it appears at first sight. Yet it is one of the most instructive chapters of the New Testament, provided one knows how to read it properly. This conclusion of the letter is particularly significant for the reason that it comes at the end of the "Letter to the Romans", the greatest, the richest and hardest piece of doctrinal writing in the whole Bible; in short, the one which comes nearest to a system of dogma. It is one and the same Paul who penned the 15 preceding chapters and this 16th chapter, and the one is as important to him as the other. The Christian Community consists of persons, and the most important, indeed, the only thing in the Community that matters are persons: God, Jesus Christ, the Holy Spirit and Christian people. The relationship of these persons to one another—that alone is essential in the Christian Community; it does not concern things or doctrines in themselves. Even the doctrines deal with the relations between persons, namely the negative and positive relation, with sin and grace. Thus, also, the personal relations of the apostle to the Communities, to the individual members of these Communities, are not a matter of secondary importance but belong to the substance of the letter. Neither Paul himself nor his message are too great for such personal greetings.

Yet these salutations not only reflect what the letter is about; they actually are this, for they are the effects and demonstrations of love, of that love which is the greatest of all the gifts of the Holy Spirit. They are also the subject in question, because in them the Christian Community becomes perceptible as reality. That is the new life, that is the "Communion of Saints"; a relationship to one another, as becomes apparent in the greetings. They are not simply greetings but a mutual meeting of one another in Christ; the individual persons are felt, each in his place, as members of the one body of which the apostle himself is a member.

And there is yet another important thing about this list of salutations: the entire Community appears in it as an active whole in which each one fulfils his worthwhile service, a community that consists, so to speak, of nothing but apostles. To be sure, they are not called apostles and the difference between the apostles and the other members of the Community continues to be observed; yet when we see that Andronicus and Junias, who are completely unknown to us, are described as apostles, then we are also being shown, as in the whole conclusion of the letter, that there could be in any case no question of some hierarchical distinction between apostles and non-apostles in the community of Paul.

The impression which these salutations make is that of a great family on the one hand and of a working community on the other, both of which are based not on natural relations but solely "in Christ" and his message. One also notices nothing of a depreciation of women such as, for instance, has been read out of the 14th chapter of 1st Corinthians; for the apostle expressly emphasizes that Phoebe rendered assistance not only to many others but also to himself, and he also calls the mother of Rufus his own "mother". Prisca, ready for martyrdom, he salutes as his fellow-worker before her husband Aquila, together with whom she presides at a house Church; along with these two most important women he also mentions Mary, Persis,

Tryphosa and Tryphaena as industrious workers "in the Lord" and besides them, with or without name, individually or together with men, he refers to a number of others. How little the apostle is concerned with stressing particularly his rank of apostleship becomes also evident from his special reference to Andronicus and Junias by saying that they had become Christians before him. He also calls special attention to his Jewish kinsmen—almost in veneration—within the Community, as a confirmation of what he mentioned in chapters 9-11 regarding his relations towards his people. The recommendation with which he introduces his fellow-worker, Phoebe, to the Community of Rome allows us also to catch a glimpse of the mutual relations of foresight and provident care within the young Church as a world-embracing fellowship. All in all, what a new aspect of the world at that time this catalogue of greetings reveals to us! what a mirror it holds up before our present day Church!

FINAL EXHORTATIONS (16: 17-20)

[17]I appeal to you, brethren, to take note of those who create dissensions and difficulties, in opposition to the doctrine which you have been taught; avoid them. [18]For such persons do not serve our Lord Christ, but their own appetites, and by fair and flattering words they deceive the hearts of the simpleminded. [19]For while your obedience is known to all, so that I rejoice over you, I would have you wise as to what is good and guileless as to what is evil; [20]then the God of peace will soon crush Satan under your feet. The grace of our Lord Jesus Christ be with you.

The series of salutations is suddenly interrupted by a warning against those who endanger the unity of the Community. The apostle is bringing all his weight into play against them; slaves of appetite, not servants of Christ, deceitful, fine talkers, tools of Satan, he calls them. We do not exactly know what teachers of erroneous doctrines are meant here. Yet we also notice here that Paul, where he sees the Community in danger from within, proceeds as ruthlessly as a surgeon who decides to remove the growth in time and radically before it fatally injures the organism. Where the corruption of Satan becomes noticeable there is no room for pity. Yet this warning has not been prompted by fear. The Romans stood firm in the faith, so that at the end they are once more held up as exemplary models. The Community, therefore, will with God's help master the infiltrating evil power. But it is just their faith, over which the apostle rejoices, that might be abused by the cunning adversary, and therefore they have need of special watchfulness.

Thus what has been impressed in detail on the individual members in earlier chapters also applies to the Community as a whole: he who stands must take care lest he fall. Even in the community with the strongest faith the dry rot of heresy may set in; it, too, must watch and pray that it may continue to preserve what it has received.

THE COMPANIONS OF THE APOSTLE (16: 21-24)

²¹Timothy, my fellow worker, greets you; so do Lucius and Jason and Sosipater, my kinsmen.

²²I Tertius, the writer of this letter, greet you in the Lord.

²³Gaius, who is host to me and to the whole church, greets you. Erastus, the city treasurer, and our brother Quartus, greet you.

[²⁴The grace of our Lord Jesus Christ be with you all. Amen. *Omitted in R.S.V.*]

Paul has already mentioned in verse 16 all Communities that join him in his greetings. Now there follow several individuals by name: Timothy, the co-founder of the Community at Corinth; Erastus, the city treasurer; Gaius, one of the few whom Paul himself had baptized (1 Cor. 1: 14), and who obviously in a special way has placed his house at their disposal for meetings. Paul's secretary, to whom he dictated the letter, is allowed to insert a greeting with his own hand. It is highly probable that Paul's letter concludes with the short blessing following this salutation and that the longer praise which now forms the end is a later addition; it is absent from several old manuscripts.

THE PRAISE OF GOD (16: 25-27)

²⁵Now to him who is able to strengthen you according to my gospel and the preaching of Jesus Christ, according to the

revelation of the mystery which was kept secret for long ages
[26]but is now disclosed and through the prophetic writings is
made known to all nations, according to the command of the
eternal God, to bring about obedience to the faith—[27]to the
only wise God be glory for evermore through Jesus Christ!
Amen.

Even if these verses are not from the hand of the apostle
Paul himself, they are still, however, a powerful recapitulation
of what was important for him in the letter—God's honour;
it is the reason and goal of all proclamation and teaching. He
alone is the teacher, the only wise God. For his will had been
unknown to mankind throughout its entire history until it
pleased him to reveal the secret and to break the silence
through the Gospel of Jesus Christ. It concerns the delivery of
this message in the name of God; for only where God is known
as he reveals himself, can one obey him, and only where one
is obedient to him does one serve his honour. God's honour and
obedience through faith, both one in Jesus Christ—that is the
message of the apostle Paul.

Appendix

APPENDIX

Some Leading Ideas in the Teaching of the Apostle Paul

RESURRECTION

SPIRIT AND FLESH

THE RIGHTEOUSNESS OF GOD

THE LAW AND THE WORKS
   OF THE LAW

FAITH

GRACE

SANCTIFICATION

JESUS CHRIST

THE CHURCH, THE COMMUNITY

LOVE

PREDESTINATION, ELECTION

THE JUSTIFICATION OF THE
   SINNER

SIN

BAPTISM

THE WRATH OF GOD AND
   RECONCILIATION

THE reason for this appendix is a twofold one. Its purpose is to show the leading ideas of the letter to the Romans in their own context and in the context of the whole of the Pauline teaching; it is also meant at the same time to serve as a bridge leading across to our own problems and to translate into the idiom of our own time what Paul is saying in the language of his day. That is the reason why the several hundred scriptural passages quoted will not always at first sight fit into the context in which they are found, but need further thought. Of the many scriptural texts to be considered only some few at a time have been selected as examples.

RESURRECTION

The entire message of the apostle, one might almost say, is the message of the resurrection. And this in a double sense: first, on the resurrection everything else depends. "But if there is no resurrection of the dead, then Christ has not been raised; if Christ has not been raised, then our preaching is in vain and your faith is in vain" (1 Cor. 15: 13-14). Thus one cannot have the Christian Faith and yet leave "this one part" out; rather everything else is nothing if there is nothing in the resurrection. Secondly, it is talking of the new life, the new "world era" which has begun with Jesus Christ (Col. 1: 13). But the actual beginning and therefore the basis of this new life is the resurrection of Jesus (Col. 1: 18). "The Theology of the Resurrection" would be no bad title for the teaching of Paul.

This decisive importance of the resurrection can only be grasped if one sees it in connection with the fact of sin and death, as Paul wants us to understand it. Death and sin belong together. With sin, death has become the ruler over mankind (Rom. 5: 12ff.). There is a "triumvirate" for Paul, a threefold firm of the anti-God power: sin, law, death (cp. 1 Cor. 15: 56). These three designate the condition of the unredeemed man; he lives in sin, under the law, in death. Therefore death is never merely the "being no longer alive", the stopping of the blood circulation and the subsequent decomposition of the body. Death for Paul is always an outward form of the evil power. "The last enemy to be destroyed is death" (1 Cor. 15: 26). Hence death has its seat in the present life and there brings forth its fruit. Where men live in sin, in godlessness, under the Law, there death is, as it were, their employer for whom they work (Rom. 6: 16ff.). His is the profit (Rom. 6: 23). Death is therefore to be understood as being anything but "natural", it is an intruder into God's Creation (Rom. 5: 12).

Correspondingly the resurrection of the dead is not merely a re-awakening to life but the complete transformation of the world and life (Phil. 3: 21; 1 Cor. 15: 23ff.). It began with the resurrection of Jesus; it is the breaking through of the life of God into the world of death (Col. 1: 18). Without the message of the resurrection of Jesus, that of his redeeming death is nothing (1 Cor. 15: 17). Good Friday was at first a complete end, a catastrophe which threatened to break the faith of the disciples entirely. Only the appearances of the risen Lord, which Paul enumerates in detail (1 Cor. 15: 3ff.), brought the disciples back from despair (Luke 24: 13ff.). But these appearances gave their faith a true clarity and depth. The meeting with the risen Lord is the real establishing of the Christian Community (Acts 1: 4). Not only that: life, the union with the Risen One, the present living Lord, is now the new life not merely of the apostles but of the entire Community of Christ (Col. 1: 27). It is the source of its power and joy and the link joining them together (1 Cor. 12: 17; Eph. 4: 15).

The life of faith is a life in and with the ever present, living, risen and exalted Lord (Gal. 2: 20). The Community shares in the resurrection of Christ; it is a question, not only of one's "believing in the resurrection", but of every single person having communion through faith with Jesus Christ (2 Cor. 13: 5). As everyone has to enter into the death of Jesus by repentance, that is, to understand and accept Christ's death as his own—the old man must die with Christ—so everyone may now also rise with him to a new life (Rom. 6: 4, 11). "Therefore if anyone is in Christ, he is a new creation; the old has passed away, the new has come" (2 Cor. 5: 17). True Christian life is resurrection-life, life in the new being of the Spirit (Rom. 8: 1ff.). As the old life led to death, carrying in everything the seed of death, so the new life leads to eternal life and has, so to speak, the seed of life in it (Rom. 8: 11; 1 John 3: 9). Of course, this new life, the resurrection-life, is still engaged in the conflict with the old and must therefore be continually fought for; it is not simply there as a matter of course, for it must continually be appropriated anew in obedience and defended against the old nature (Rom. 6: 11ff.). To this new life, therefore, the life of the resurrection, belong two things which indicate its present incompleteness: we are told to walk in this new life (Rom. 6: 4) and we only hope for the actual, full resurrection that will deliver us from "this body of death" (Rom. 2: 24; 8: 11).

Thus it is understandable that wherever Paul speaks of being risen with Christ, he refers to it with great joy and assurance of victory but at the same time with restraint, as something only present in the state of becoming and only in its incomplete and veiled form (Rom. 8: 23ff.). It is so far a life still "hid with Christ in God" (Col. 3: 3), and we still wait for the resurrection in which Christ has gone before us as the "first fruits of those who have fallen asleep" (1 Cor. 15: 20). That he has gone before us is the pledge of our being permitted to follow him; that he has gone before us means that we are not yet there, where he is. Yet he has indeed gone before us to blaze the trail for us. What has happened to him is also to happen to us (1 Cor. 15: 12ff.). We are "sealed" (2 Cor. 1: 22; Eph. 4: 30) for this heavenly inheritance. We are those who look for the entire, all-transforming resurrection which is bound up with his coming again in glory (1 Cor. 15: 21ff.).

Paul's teaching about this our resurrection is not entirely unambiguous. He indeed knows that it will be a complete end of the old and a complete beginning of the new, for the corruptible cannot inherit the incorruptible (1 Cor. 15: 50). And yet he simultaneously hopes that "not all will have to sleep" (1 Cor. 15: 51) before this last thing comes about; that at least some, perhaps he himself, may "not be unclothed" but rather "further clothed" (2 Cor. 5: 4), that is to say, that this new world era will break into his present lifetime. It seems as if towards the end of his life Paul said something different about himself from what he said in his earlier years (cp. Phil. 1: 23 with 1 Thess. 4: 17). He also takes over the Jewish conception of a universal resurrection in which all, even unbelievers, somehow have a share in order to be brought before the judgment seat of God (Rom. 2: 8; 2 Thess. 1: 9). Yet he also knows that just in these things we must remember that our knowledge here is imperfect, like seeing through a mirror dimly (1 Cor. 13: 12). The "how" remains a mystery and beyond imagination, but the "that" is certain. This applies especially to everything which we say regarding the life eternal. Paul exercises in this the utmost restraint. There is no trace of the heavenly glory. The full redemption in which even death as the last enemy will be abolished (1 Cor. 15: 26) is certain; there is no doubt that for those who belong already to Christ eternal life is prepared (Phil. 3: 10ff.; Col. 3: 4), and none either that "God will be all and in all' (1 Cor. 15: 28). Paul, however, does not go beyond such hints and we, too, ought obviously not to do so either.

SPIRIT AND FLESH

1. *The Human Spirit*

For Paul, as for the whole Bible, man is a unity. No doubt, body and spirit (1 Cor. 7: 34; Eph. 4: 4) or even body, soul and spirit must be distinguished (1 Thess. 5: 23). But much more important than this difference is the homogeneity of these two or three elements, making up that unity of the person which is summed up by the "heart". Where the person as a whole acts or suffers from the depth and centre of his being this is "in the heart" or "with the heart" (Rom. 10: 10; Phil. 1: 7). The spirit is not, as with the Greek philosophers or in modern thought, especially emphasized, for there can be no question here of the spirit being the divine part of man. Just as little does one find in Paul an "immortal soul". The assurance of eternity too, rather applies to the whole man—resurrection of the body as well as of the soul (Rom. 8: 11; 1 Cor. 15: 38; Phil. 3: 21)—and is not, for instance, based on the eternity of the spirit or the soul but quite solely on God's redeeming, new-creating act (compare *Resurrection*). Paul, of course, includes in spirit the mental activities of thought and conscious, purposive will (1 Cor. 2: 11ff.). In so far as the turning away from God, which is sin, is based on these, it is then precisely the spirit which is the part responsible for evil (Rom. 2: 29; 2 Cor. 7: 1). Yet we shall do better to say: the whole man, in person, is responsible as the body-soul unity.

2. *The Flesh*

Thus what Paul means by flesh cannot be accurately rendered by "body" or "the lower faculties", or "the sensual life" and similar phrases. Flesh is rather an expression designating man as a whole; namely, according to his creatureliness (Gal. 2: 16; 3: 3). Flesh is man as the one who without God's aid is impotent, futile (Rom. 6: 19; 8: 3, 12). What is more, however, flesh for Paul is also human existence turned away from God, and hence sinful (Rom. 8: 7, 13). For us to-day this is a strange idiom only comprehensible from Hebrew. But it is profoundly significant. He wants to say: the man who wishes to live from himself, the man who does not understand himself through God but as a being living from himself, is, so to speak, only a part of the world, a powerless thing which one best thinks of in conjunction with the body distinct from the Spirit (Rom. 7: 23, 25). Thus the concept flesh appears in differing colours in "physical nature", "creatureliness" and "sinfulness" (Rom. 7: 18). To rely on the flesh, to trust in it or "to walk after the flesh" does not mean, for instance, to surrender to sensuality, the lower appetites, but to live in a worldly manner, godlessly, taking heed only of the creature (2 Cor. 11: 18; Gal. 6: 13) —even though in the highest spirituality of art and science (1 Cor. 1: 26-29). The opposite to it is "after the Spirit" or "walking in the Spirit" and by this is meant the same thing as

the life in Christ or being determined and moved by the Holy
Spirit (Rom. 8: 1ff.).

3. *The Holy Spirit*

The Holy Spirit is God's Spirit or the Spirit of Christ (Rom.
8: 9; 2 Cor. 3: 17). He is never our own spirit (Rom. 8: 16).
And Paul certainly never speaks of this Spirit of God as is
occasionally the case in the Old Testament; namely, as the
creative Spirit of God ruling over all created things, bestowing
and upholding life. He speaks of this Holy Spirit always and
only in connection with Jesus Christ, with the redeeming power
of God penetrating through faith in the Gospel into the old life
as a new and renewing strength (Rom. 8: 1ff.; 2 Cor. 3: 3ff.).
Indeed one may almost designate the Spirit as "the new life"
(Rom. 8: 9ff.). Thus he is also God's Spirit, but the Spirit of
God as strength and power of the new life among believers and
in the Community (Gal. 5: 5, 16).

Without faith, without Jesus Christ, we are cut off from God,
flesh and fleshly, powerless to do good, abandoned to sin and
death (Rom. 7: 5ff.; 8: 13). Through faith, however, we partake of the new world, the heavenly existence, even share in the
life of God (1 Cor. 2: 10; 12: 11; Eph. 2: 22). But we must
notice that Paul never says we receive faith through the Holy
Spirit, but always that we receive the Holy Spirit through faith
(Gal. 3: 2; Rom. 5: 5). To be sure, it is God who creates faith
through the message of Jesus Christ (Rom. 10: 17; Col. 2: 12),
causing it to sink into the heart and apprehending us through it
(Phil. 3: 12). Yet it is only in consequence of our being apprehended in this way that we receive the Holy Spirit, just as we
only partake of the new life in this way (Rom. 5: 5; 2 Cor. 4:
12f.; Gal. 3: 14). The Spirit is that element of the heavenly life
which we receive already now as a "pledge" or first fruits
(2 Cor. 1: 22; 5: 5; Eph. 1: 13f.).

But neither is this act of receiving to be thought of as having
some natural-magical quality. We must walk, think, will and
strive "according to the Spirit" (Rom. 8: 1, 4; 12: 8). The
Spirit does not come upon us like a natural happening, but he
remains bound to our entirely personal conduct, thinking and
willing (1 Cor. 14: 14, 16; Gal. 5: 5). To be sure, the Spirit
"dwells" in believers (Rom. 8: 9; 1 Cor. 3: 16) yet they can

again become separated from him through sin and thus lose him (Gal. 5: 17; Eph. 4: 30). But provided they walk "according to the Spirit" (Rom. 8: 4) the Spirit shows himself in them as a creative power by his fruits (Eph. 5: 9), which are clearly and recognizably different from the fruits of the flesh (Gal. 5: 22), so that one is able to test whether one is walking in the Spirit or in the flesh (2 Cor. 13: 5), even whether another person is walking in the Spirit or in the flesh (2 Cor. 13: 6; 1 Cor. 2: 4; 1 John 4: 1). Even though this test may not hit the mark with absolute certainty, since God alone is the infallible knower of the heart (1 Thess. 2: 4; 1 Cor. 4: 4), this testing is still commanded us, both as self-examination (Gal. 6: 4; 2 Cor. 13: 5) and as the examination of others (1 Thess. 3: 5; 2 Cor. 12: 20f.).

Just as the Spirit is the carrier and producer of the new life, so is he also of the new freedom (2 Cor. 3: 18). There is only the either—or: either one lives under the law or one lives in the Spirit (Gal. 5: 18; Rom. 7: 6). If one lives under the law, one brings forth the fruits of death (Rom. 6: 14, 21); if one lives in the Spirit, one has the fruits of life (Rom. 6: 22). If one lives under the law, one is not free, for the law is an enslaving power (Gal. 4: 1-5). If one lives by the Spirit, one is free (Rom. 8: 21); for where the Spirit is, there is freedom (2 Cor. 3: 17; Rom. 8: 2; Gal. 5: 1ff.). But it is the freedom of those who are totally bound in union with their Lord (2 Cor. 3: 18). It is the freedom of the free obedience of love (Gal. 5: 13; Rom. 6: 22).

It is the Spirit, too, who liberates one from anxiety (Rom. 8: 15f.) and who together with the peace of God brings also great joy, even the rejoicing of God's children, into the heart (Gal. 5: 22; Rom. 8: 21). The Spirit is the direct bond with God Himself (1 Cor. 2: 10ff.; 6: 17). That which is apprehended by the Spirit is snatched away from death as it is snatched away from sin (Rom. 8: 2). Therefore the indwelling of the Holy Spirit in us is already the beginning of eternal life in this earthly existence (Phil. 1: 21; Rom. 8: 10). God and Spirit, Jesus Christ and Spirit form a trilateral unity (2 Cor. 13: 13). The mystery of the triune God is not further discussed either by Paul or in the New Testament in general, but only just touched upon (1 Cor. 12: 4-6). It is not possible to speak here of the manifold gifts of the Spirit. Everything that emerges as new in the life of the Christian and the Christian Community is the gift of the Spirit (cp. 1 Cor. 12-14), even many things which we may not be able to understand at first or cannot appreciate so positively as Paul (1 Cor. 14: 5ff.). But he also distinguishes between what builds up the community and what belongs rather to the private life of the individual (1 Cor. 14: 4). And he declares with unmistakable clarity that the most important gift of the Spirit is love—that love which does not seek its own (1 Cor. 2: 31).

THE RIGHTEOUSNESS OF GOD

By "righteousness" the Bible always understands something more than our use of the word, which is determined by legal concepts. We come closer to the biblical thought when we say: "Being righteous". It is the endeavour of the pious Jew to be righteous. But that means especially to be in such a state that God acknowledges one as righteous at the judgment. The pious Jew thought he could gain this righteousness through the works of the Law, whereas man to-day thinks, in regard to "being righteous", less of God's judgment than of the verdict of his fellow-men and the verdict of his own conscience. Paul now shows that that, taken seriously, cannot avail any man (Rom. 3: 10ff.). Every man is a sinner (Rom. 3: 23). That does not mean he does only evil, but it implies that he does always evil, that evil, opposition to God, is always present in his deeds (Rom. 2-3). One's own righteousness, therefore, is an illusion (Gal. 2: 16).

But now Paul knows another kind, the righteousness or justice of God (Rom. 1: 17; 3: 21). He does not understand by it what we think of first when hearing the word, namely that God judges "impartially", "uniformly", "without respect of person". Paul rather understands by the righteousness of God, along with the Old Testament, the sovereign will of God. God is righteous in so far as he asserts his will, be it through judgment or grace (Rom. 3: 25). God as righteous is the One who makes right, who causes something to become righteous—be it a man or a people, a relation or a condition (2 Cor. 5: 21; Eph. 4: 24).

From this we have to understand now the particular application of the expression "the righteousness of God" in the letter to the Romans. Through the Law and the works of the Law God's will cannot really assert its authority. Men do not thereby really become righteous. The Law overcomes sin but not opposition to God's will (Rom. 3: 20). God therefore himself intervenes. He sends his Son who does his will (Rom. 5: 18) and who by his death unites anew, "reconciles", man with God (Col. 1: 20ff.). God removes sin by cancelling the debt through the sacrifice of his Son (Rom. 3: 25; Col. 2: 14) and by forgiveness makes peace with him (Eph. 2: 12, 14). God annuls the debt (Col. 2: 14) and thereby establishes a new relation between himself and men, that of sonship (Gal. 4: 5). He declares that men are "righteous" for him as soon as they believe it.

In accepting from God this new status in relationship, this righteousness that is bestowed, man has it and is a righteous man (Rom. 3: 26; Gal. 3: 24). Through faith he is now one who is right with God, one in whom God's will asserts its authority. For God desires only one thing: that men shall know themselves wholly dependent on him, that they shall live entirely by his giving (Rom. 10: 10). When that happens, that is, where men let the righteousness of God be given to them, there they are righteous, there they possess the "righteousness of God" (Rom. 3: 21; 10: 3). Thus Paul can speak alternately of the righteousness of God and the righteousness of faith (Rom. 4: 13; 3: 21f.). The two are the same, seen from two sides. God's righteouness wants to say: being righteous comes from God alone. He it is who establishes the new relationship between himself and men; he declares that they are right with him. But the righteousness of faith says: this righteousness becomes ours through faith, and that means simply by receiving it, by allowing it to be bestowed upon oneself.

THE LAW AND THE WORKS OF THE LAW

The struggle against the "works of the Law" is the one main theme of the letter to the Romans. Properly to distinguish between Law and Gospel, or Law and Faith, or Law and Promise is, according to Luther, the most important thing in all Christian knowledge. What is to be understood by that?

The Law is first of all quite simply the demand of God made

known to man. Therefore the Law itself is holy, divine, good (Rom. 7: 12-14). It comes from God (Rom. 7: 25). Paul here is partly thinking of everything commanded in the books of the law of the Old Testament, but partly also of the command of love as the sum or meaning of all laws (Rom. 13: 10). He thus takes account of the fact that the Gentiles, too, know something of the Law (Rom. 2: 15) and even do the works of the Law (Rom. 2: 14). For they also know of something that one ought and ought not to do (Rom. 1: 32).

What then is wrong with the Law, that Paul has to fight against it as against an enemy of God—yes, as against an enemy more dangerous than all others?

Properly speaking Paul never fights against the Law: only against man living under the Law (Gal. 3: 12f., 21). For the Law makes man in a wrong way independent over against God. The works of the Law are one's own works; the man who does the works of the Law believes that he can boast before God, thus thinking himself entitled to God's praise and God's reward (Rom. 3: 27; 1 Cor. 1: 29). He believes he is able to do good in his own strength and thus to be good. The Law has for man, just as he is, namely for sinful man, the result that he relies on his own action and thinks he is able to win God's favour through his own moral or religious effort (Rom. 9: 31; Gal. 3: 10). Now Paul does not in the least argue that man cannot fulfil individual commandments, that is isolated parts of the Law, so to speak (Phil. 3: 6). On the contrary, he expressly admits this (Rom. 2: 14); yet he says: whoever takes up his position on the basis of the Law, whoever stands in a legal relation to God, must fulfil the whole Law (Gal. 5: 3; 3: 10). No instalment system or part payment here! God's Law needs to be fulfilled completely; any disobedience against God's Law is damning, destructive in its consequences (Gal. 3: 10). It makes man a debtor who deserves death. Therefore the Law causes wrath (Rom. 4: 15); that is, it places every man under God's judgment of condemnation (Rom. 3: 8; 2 Cor. 3: 9). It is thus not a way of salvation but of disaster.

In Jesus Christ God opens up quite another way, the way of grace or faith (Rom. 3: 21ff.). But hence it becomes also recognizable that the way of the Law is not the one originally shown by God. The Law has "come in between" (Rom. 5: 20;

Gal. 3: 19); the Law, we can therefore say, is God's will as sinful man understands it (Gal. 3: 19). Faith understands God's will quite differently. It is part of the sinful understanding of God when man thinks he must and can become righteous of himself; he does not know that the true, the only real righteousness is that granted by God. The legally-minded man is thus "man in his own strength", the religious or moral self-made man; this self-awareness, this glorifying himself separates him from God more than anything else, for it makes him independent of God (Rom. 10: 3). The legally-minded man does not notice that, by wanting to be good himself, he actually denies the one thing that is good: dependence on God. Thus we can also say conversely: everything that makes man independent over against God, everything that makes him conscious of his own ability and his own worth in independence from God, all that is Law in the sense of being the works of the Law. Legalism is man's relying on himself over against God. Righteousness by the Law is self-righteousness and therefore of necessity leads to self-glorification. Self-praise in the face of God is the height of folly and delusion (1 Cor. 4: 7; 1: 29).

And yet Paul does not appraise the Law merely negatively. Within God's plan it is important in a twofold connection. It has first a protecting significance (Gal. 3: 23). It protects man from the worst moral and religious carelessness. It keeps him in a way close to God, thus having a preparatory task in respect of the message of Christ. It is the schoolmaster bringing to Christ (Gal. 3: 24). And secondly, from the Law springs the knowledge of sin (Rom. 3: 20). If we keep before us God's holy will, it can—if God grants it—lead to our eyes being opened to our sin, so that we recognize and note our irreconcilable guilt, that our duty towards God can never be put aside and that this way only leads to the abyss (Rom. 7: 7ff.; Gal. 3: 10).

But for him who lives in faith, in grace, in Christ, in the Spirit, the Law is annulled (Gal. 4: 4). He stands in quite a different relation to God (Gal. 5: 18). The will of God is now inscribed in his heart, love now urges him on to do God's will (2 Cor. 5: 14). God's will no longer confronts him as an alien law, for the believer is, as one reconciled to God, united with him; he no longer requires the Law, because God's Spirit has become the leader in him, showing him God's will (Rom. 8:

14). Whereas the Law was incapable of moving the man to action, to whom it presented the will of God (Rom. 8: 3), the Spirit of God Himself is the power of the good and the will to the good which leads to action (Rom. 8: 4ff.; Gal. 5: 6).

FAITH

The meaning of the word faith has changed so much that one is hardly able to use it any longer as a translation of the Greek word *pistis*. Yet something of the old meaning still lingers in the expression "fidelity and faith". In the Bible, and especially for Paul, the meaning of fidelity or trust stands in the foreground. Faith is a relationship of fidelity between two persons. He who "has faith" in the Lord or believes "in" God (Rom. 4: 3, 5) is united with him in fidelity and joined to him in his whole person. Faith for Paul is first and foremost not faith "in something" but faith "in someone", in God, in Jesus Christ (Gal. 2: 16; Rom. 3: 22, 26). Faith is trust, entrusting oneself to someone, and obedience. Paul often uses the word obedience as a synonym for faith (Rom. 15: 18; 6: 17) or from the two he coins the expression "obedience of faith" (Rom. 1: 5).

Above all, faith is the trust and obedience with which man encounters Jesus Christ, in whom God reveals himself and descends to humanity (Rom. 3: 25). Faith is the receiving of God's grace, forgiveness and reconciliation in Jesus Christ (Gal. 2: 20; Rom. 3: 22ff.). Faith trusts in the fidelity, mercy and love of God which he shows in Jesus Christ to sinful and unfaithful man (Eph. 2: 5-8; Rom. 5: 6ff.). Thus faith has fundamentally nothing to do with a doctrine or an article of faith, but with God Himself in his self-revelation (Gal. 2: 20). But now this revelation of God happens in such a way that the message, the Gospel of Jesus Christ is proclaimed to us (Rom. 1: 16; 1 Thess. 2: 13). We have to be told who Jesus Christ is, and what God intends to give us in him (Rom. 8: 32). God's gift, which we receive by faith, is Jesus Christ Himself (Rom. 5: 15ff.); but it comes to us through the Word (Rom. 10: 8, 17). Thus Jesus is also called—by John not by Paul (John 1: 14)— the incarnate Word. Message and matter for Paul are one; in the message, in the Gospel, God stretches out to us his saving

hand and faith clasps it in trust and obedience as God's hand
(Rom. 1: 16). Man trusts—entrusts himself obediently to this
saving will of God which meets him in the Gospel (1 Cor. 1: 21;
Gal. 3: 22). Therefore faith is also faith in the Word of God
(Rom. 10: 8; Phil. 2: 16); but it is never a question of assenting
to a dogma, a doctrine in and for itself, for faith is precisely
this—that one perceives in the message God Himself, Jesus
Christ Himself (2 Cor. 5: 19ff.).

Jesus Christ to whom faith refers is God's act of salvation
(Rom. 3: 25; Col. 2: 12f.). Faith is allowing this act of salvation
to happen to oneself (Col. 1: 13, 14, 21-23). It is in the first place
a pure receiving, a being seized by Christ (Phil. 3: 12). Yet at
the same time faith is, as an act of trust and obedience, anything but "passive". It is a decision for God (Phil. 1: 27-29);
it is thus indeed bestowed by God (Rom. 12: 3; Col. 2: 12),
but is neverthess demanded by God (Rom. 11: 31; Eph. 6:
16). It is a gift from God and yet man's personal answer to
God's Word (Rom. 4: 19; 10: 9). Certain though it is, however,
that faith is also an act of man, it is yet never an achievement
for which God owes man an acknowledgment or reward.
When it says that faith is "reckoned" as righteousness (Rom.
4: 5ff.) Paul merely wants to give expression to the incomprehensible fact that God accounts something to man which he
himself has granted (Gal. 3: 18). The relation of faith is thus
one where, seen from man, every claim ceases, since everything
rests solely on God's mercy (Rom. 9: 15f.; 11: 32). That which
God "accounts" to man is his own gift. Here reckoning up, and
hence self-glorification, comes to an end (Rom. 3: 27).

Faith stands in an indissoluble relationship with two other
great things: with hope and with love (1 Cor. 13: 13).

First *with hope*: for what God bestows on man by faith is
above all a new outlook (Rom. 5: 2ff.), the assurance of full
redemption (Rom. 8: 38), the expectation of the eternal inheritance (Gal. 3: 29). As faith looks upward—from man and
from everything that is human and earthly to the heavenly
Lord (Phil. 3: 20)—so it also looks forward, to the final realization of God's reign in the world of the resurrection (Col. 3: 4;
Phil. 3: 10).

Secondly *with love*: for faith is nothing less than being
apprehended by the love of God (Eph. 3: 17). Faith and

being placed in the divine love are one and the same thing (Gal. 2: 20). Through faith, love is kindled in our hearts, that love which does not seek its own (1 Cor. 3: 5; Eph. 5: 2). These two are so closely and necessarily connected with one another that nothing counts "save faith alone working through love" (Gal. 5: 6). Love is therefore greater than faith, since faith itself is only the vessel of love (1 Cor. 13: 13). God is love, not faith (1 John 4: 16). Faith is the receiving of God's love, which is itself life, eternal life.

GRACE

There is hardly a concept of the Bible which has suffered as badly as this one in the later development of Christian teaching. Grace, like almost all the important words of the New Testament, is a personal term, more exactly a word denoting a personal relationship. Grace is God's condescending to man (Tit. 2: 11), who is not worthy of it but stands in need of it (Rom. 4: 25; 2 Cor. 8: 9). Grace is the love of God, with the additional meaning that it is immotivated giving and unmerited love (Rom. 3: 24, 9: 12; Eph. 2: 5ff.), love "without any cause", "simply because God wills it so" (Rom. 9: 15). Grace therefore stands in the sharpest contrast to "merit" (Rom. 11: 6) and to everything achieved and gained by oneself (Gal. 2: 21; Eph. 2: 8). Grace always denotes that which comes from God. It is thus in Paul's message actually almost identical with Jesus Christ (Rom. 5: 2, 15). He is the great gift; indeed, rightly understood, he is the great giving of God (Rom. 5: 15ff.). For Jesus Christ is truly a person, yet he is above all God's gift (Eph. 1: 5ff.). Jesus Christ is God's bestowing hand, God's acquitting word, God's saving arm; in Jesus Christ God's eye beholds us mercifully and graciously. He is the Grace of God in person.

The thought underlying grace is always that of judicial verdict. Grace is pardon, acquittal from that punishment which we deserved by right and which would be to our eternal ruin (Rom. 3: 24f.). Grace therefore is also exemption from merited condemnation (Rom. 5: 16). Yet Paul is careful never to leave it in this merely negative form. Grace is never merely the setting aside of condemnation but the royal bestowal of gifts at the banquet; the granting of the highest good, eternal life (Rom. 5: 21). Of course, grace, like faith, leads only to the threshold of this last thing of all, the divine glory (2 Cor. 5: 7; 12: 9).

SANCTIFICATION

The word holy is a key word of the Bible and also of the Pauline proclamation. Holiness is God's way of being (1 Pet. 1: 16). Apart from God, holiness can only be spoken of, for example, in reference to man, the Community, the temple and so forth, in so far as God stands in a particular relationship with them, and, especially, in so far as God singles them out for his service. Thus for Paul the Christian believers are almost always "the saints" because they are the chosen ones of God (Rom. 1: 6f.), those who are called by him into fellowship with him through Christ (1 Cor. 1: 9) and because they share in this way, through the Holy Spirit, in God's life which is holy (1 Cor. 3: 17). They are holy because, through justification, they are taken out of their separation from God (Col. 1: 12ff.) and transferred into the realm of God, into fellowship with God (1 Cor. 1: 9; Eph. 2: 19). The justified are, as such, also the holy (1 Cor. 6: 11; Eph. 1: 4).

Yet we understand this statement only in the sense of the apostle Paul if we bear in mind that justification, for him, is never merely forgiveness which blots out the guilt of sin, so cancelling the separation from God—although this is the first thing—(Rom. 3: 24ff.) but that it is at the same time setting right, the making righteous, in that with the declaration of righteousness the Holy Spirit becomes operative in man, transforming the life which was godless and hostile to God into one that is in harmony with God and well-pleasing to him (1 Cor. 6: 11). Justification also includes sanctification (Eph. 5: 26).

Thus it is God alone who sanctifies (1 Thess. 5: 23). Only he has holiness, only he can bestow it, and he does so by giving his Son and his Spirit and in him the new life (1 Cor. 1: 30; Rom. 8: 1ff.). This new life, however, is always also a new will with a new conduct flowing from it, a new activity (Rom. 8: 12). Therefore sanctification is not solely God's gift but at the same time man's task (Rom. 6: 19-22). Paul tells his communities that everyone is to sanctify himself (2 Cor. 7: 1; Rom. 12: 1). The usage of the word holy is also rooted entirely in biblical thought (Lev. 19: 2). God does not thrust the new life at anyone; it must be appropriated by every man acting himself. Sanctification takes place through God, but it happens only in that man, by his obedience of faith, offers his life and his members to God for this sanctification, just as the sick person stretches out his diseased limb to the surgeon for the operation (Rom. 12: 1; 6: 13, 19). It therefore takes place entirely through God's Spirit alone (Rom. 15: 16). Yet it happens by the requisition of the human will and thought (2 Cor. 7: 1; Rom. 6: 19). And it must penetrate through everything in man (1 Thess. 5: 23) thus making him "blameless" or irreproachable at the end (Eph. 1: 4; 2: 21; 5: 27). Man is thus made holy in the full sense only in that and in so far as the Holy Spirit begins to operate in him and the flesh no longer acts, lives, thinks, feels and wills from its own criteria, the old man from his old nature, but that all these movements of the heart are guided by the Spirit of God (Phil. 4: 8).

The doctrine of perfection (perfectionism) therefore is as foreign to the apostle as its opposite. He knows and confesses of himself that this process of sanctification is not completed (Phil. 3: 13); yet he emphasizes still more frequently that it is mightily in operation and approaching its perfection (Col. 1: 28; 2 Thess. 1: 3ff.; Col. 1: 10f.). The new life, to be sure, is hid with Christ (Col. 3: 3), since it is a life by faith and not by sight (2 Cor. 5: 7); for Christ Himself is only present through his Word and by his Spirit and not visibly. Yet this new life must necessarily show itself in a new way of living (Rom. 8: 1ff.), in the fruits of the Spirit (Gal. 5: 22; Eph. 5: 9), by works of love (1 Thess. 4: 9), in services performed for the Community and the individual believers (Gal. 5: 13), in a new thinking, feeling and willing (Phil. 4: 8), in a new speaking (Col. 4: 6) and in a new way of living together (Eph. 5 and 6). Paul not only does not say that the fruits of the Spirit are also invisible, but he declares the exact opposite and continues to stress this (Rom. 1: 8; 1 Cor. 5: 11; Col. 1: 6; 2 Cor. 7: 4; 2 Cor. 8: 7, 6: 4ff.).

The new life has its roots entirely in what is invisible and in the "world beyond", in faith in Jesus Christ. Yet it is itself not beyond and invisible, but it is the living, creating and self evidencing presence of the Spirit (1 Cor. 15: 10; 12: 7ff.). The perfection of the new life lies in the future, in the coming of Christ in power. But the beginning and the mighty growth of the new life takes place here and now (Rom. 6: 22), in man, in the Community (Eph. 4: 15) and thus also in visibility. Thus every believer, as well as the Community as a whole, ought to examine themselves whether the life from Christ and in Christ is really in them (2 Cor. 13: 5; Gal. 6: 4). Since the obedience of faith is the turning of the whole man to God and Jesus Christ, and is to be distinguished, as the faith of the heart, from the mere faith of the mind (Rom. 10: 10), self-examination also belongs to the obedience of faith and to sanctification (1 Cor. 11: 28).

JESUS CHRIST

Jesus, the Christ, is not just one part of the Pauline pro-clamation alongside others but its one and only content (1 Cor. 2: 2). The question often heard, whether God is not thereby pushed into the background, is based on a complete misunder-standing. Of course, in faith we are concerned with God alone, with God's "righteousness" (Rom. 1: 17). But this God, the Creator of all things, the Lord and Giver of life, the Holy One and Merciful, the Ruler and the Redeemer becomes actually recognizable and near to us only in Jesus Christ (Col. 1: 26; Eph. 3: 1ff.). Of course, Paul expressly teaches that God also makes himself known in his works (Rom. 1; 19f.) and that therefore they also might be able "to know" him (Rom. 1: 21, 28) who are ignorant of Jesus Christ in his historical appearance, the Word of God who became man, the Crucified and Risen One. It is vital for Paul to say this because men's responsibility for their sin depends on this. Just because they do know something of God they are inexcusable in their ungod-liness (Rom. 1: 20). The significance of this universal know-ledge of God does not extend beyond this; in face of the power of sin it proves itself powerless. It is itself dragged into it and thus leads to idolatry (Rom. 1: 21ff.).

The Law also is a form of God's revelation; and indeed not merely the Mosaic Law, but also that which has been inscribed

upon the hearts of all men (Rom. 2: 15). All men know
something of God's will (Rom. 1: 32). Yet this knowledge out
of the Law does not create life or bring salvation. The Law
"brings wrath" (Rom. 4: 15). The man who knows God only
through the Law does not really know him and is not really
united with him. The Law demonstrates and indeed causes the
separation, it fills up the measure of sin (Rom. 7: 13). God
cannot be truly known either from Nature or from the Law in
such a way that this knowledge becomes life with God and so
salvation. What God truly is, what he wants from us and wishes
to do with us, what his intention towards us and his plan for us
is, that we only know through the revelation which happens
"apart from the Law", through Jesus Christ (Rom. 3: 21ff.;
Gal. 4: 4; Eph. 2: 6-9).

It is remarkable how little Paul has to say, especially in the
letter to the Romans, as to who Jesus Christ is. Obviously it
matters far more to the apostle to show what God does in Jesus
Christ (Rom. 3: 24; Eph. 2: 10). One can say straight out that
Jesus Christ is God's deed, God's word, God's revelation, God's
approach, God's covenant with man (Phil. 2: 5ff.; 1: 11;
1 Thess. 1: 10). He *is*—not only creates—God's righteousness,
as he is also "our righteousness" (1 Cor. 1: 30; 2 Cor. 5: 21).
This is a reminder for us that we must understand Jesus Christ
from the point of view of God's action, as God's act of salvation
(Col. 1: 13f.).

To the question: What or who is Jesus Christ? the letter to
the Romans, like the other Pauline letters, gives us only a
scanty reply. He is in the first place the "Son" of God (Rom.
1: 3f.). He came out of God's existence into the earthly existence (Phil. 2: 5ff.); he is the revealed mystery of God (Col. 1:
26f.; Eph. 1: 9; Col. 2: 2), the revealed will of God—creating
will and redeeming will—(Col. 1: 15f.); he is the One in whom
God Himself is present and acts (2 Cor. 5: 19), the original
image of God and the archetype of man which comes to the
fallen human creature, restoring him to his first state (Rom. 8:
29; Col. 1: 15; 3: 10; Eph. 4: 24). He is the One in whom God
makes known personally his own nature and will (Col. 1: 18f.),
thus freeing man, who is imprisoned in sin and law (Rom. 5:
18ff.) and recreating him (2 Cor. 5: 17; Eph. 2: 15). He is the
God who personally meets us, reconciles and redeems us in

human history (Col. 1: 27). Jesus the Christ is not beside God but God Himself in his approach to us. He is God as he discloses himself to us according to his inner, hidden nature and thus God's hand with which he grasps and draws us to himself (Gal. 1: 6; Phil. 3: 12).

Paul, therefore, does not see God and Christ as standing side by side—which we should have to meditate on further—but rather as a "sequence" in the movement descending from eternity to us and from us ascending again into eternity (Phil. 2: 5ff.; 3: 14ff.). Thus we look in vain to Paul for statements about the mutual relation of God and Jesus Christ. In Jesus we are dealing with God—that must satisfy us; with the God who has mercy on us and who of himself sets a new beginning to our life, namely the beginning of life eternal.

This Jesus Christ is, in faith, through the Holy Spirit, not past for us, a "historical" character, but alive and present (2 Cor. 13: 3ff.; Eph. 3: 17; Gal. 2: 20). Yes, even his death and his resurrection are for us through faith a living present—not in the manner of a man of the past who by a vividly historical presentation becomes "present" for us, but really and effectually present as God is present to us (Eph. 2: 5; Rom. 6: 11). Thus Paul can say both things: we are, through faith, in Christ (e.g. Rom. 6: 23) and Christ is in us (Gal. 2: 20; Col. 1: 27). When a man comes to have faith in the Gospel of the reconciliation through the Cross, there in the midst of this temporality the separating factor of time is eliminated and the division between the heavenly there and the earthly here is overcome (Phil. 3: 20), although as long as we live in this flesh we still suffer under the separation (2 Cor. 2: 5-6). Therefore Christ is the ever-living and present, reigning and quickening head of the Community (Eph. 4: 15) and the Community his body whose many members are, through him, one in him (Rom. 12: 4f.; 1 Cor. 12: 12-27). This present Christ, in whom we are one through faith, is the new life (Eph. 2: 5; Rom. 8: 2; 6: 11). It is no exaggeration and no poetical manner of speech when Paul says that Jesus Christ is his life (Phil. 1: 21). That is meant quite literally. As the natural man breathes air and lives by it, so the Christian man "breathes" Jesus Christ and lives by him and in him through faith. Faith is the living union with the living Christ (Col. 3: 4).

This union, however, is still imperfect in consequence of the separation that is created through the "sinful flesh", which faithful believers have also still to bear. Thus the coming of God is as yet not completed (Rom. 8: 23ff.). We wait for the coming of Jesus Christ which will put an end to this separation (Phil. 3: 21). Paul occasionally speaks of it in tremendously clear statements (1 Thess. 4: 14ff.; 1 Cor. 15: 23ff., 51ff.). But he also knows very well that all our imaginings do not reach the heart of the matter (1 Cor. 13: 12). We only know: he who has begun the work will also finish it (Phil. 1: 6). He who has reconciled us will also completely redeem us (Rom. 8: 11). He who came to us as a servant in the form of sinful flesh (Rom. 8: 3) will one day come in the glory of his heavenly nature (Phil. 3: 20) and turn our faith into sight (Col. 3: 4; 1 Cor. 13: 12). This day of Jesus Christ is the goal towards which everything is directed for Paul (1 Cor. 1: 8). This is God's actual intention (Eph. 4: 30), his goal for mankind and the world for which everything has been planned (Eph. 1: 10; Col. 1: 20, 28). And it is also that by which alone one is able to understand what faith and obedience are concerned with (1 Thess. 1: 9f.). What matters is to run towards this goal (Phil. 3: 14; 1 Cor. 9: 24f.) as it approaches us from the other side (1 Thess. 5: 1ff.). It is a matter of preparing oneself for the day of Jesus Christ and—as it says time and again—of becoming blameless (1 Cor. 1: 8; Phil. 1: 10). The aiming towards this goal is the driving force of the Christian life (Col. 3: 4ff.).

THE CHURCH, THE COMMUNITY

In hardly any other letter of the apostle is there so little express mention of the Community as in that to the Romans. This may be due to the fact that for him the "Community" or "Church" is not so much the *object* as the *subject* of faith. The Church, the Community—the believers themselves are that, of course (cp. the beginning and concluding sentences of his letters). Paul knows nothing of another kind of "Church", either in this or in any other of his letters. He knows nothing of the idea of the Church as an "institution", an establishment, as a constitutional order and so on. The Church is the body of Christ (Rom. 12: 5) whose individual members are the believers whose cohesive unity (Eph. 4: 4ff.) is Christ, the Lord Himself (1 Cor. 10: 16; 12: 27). "Church" is an Entirely personal concept; she consists exclusively of persons.

To be sure, the Church is more than the "sum" of believers; she is a mysterious unity, as is expressed in the metaphor of the body which is also not a total but an "organic" unity of its individual parts. She is therefore a unity because she is in Christ. Jesus Christ is the unity that binds the individual members together (Eph. 4: 15, 16). One can equally say the Holy Spirit is the binding unity (1 Cor. 12: 4ff.; Eph. 4: 4); again: it is love which unites (Eph. 4: 15). Yet the uniting element is always personal, never something neutral; no canon law, no official order or things of that kind. The Church or Community does have offices (1 Cor. 12: 28; Eph. 4: 11), she makes and requires certain ordinances (1 Cor. 14: 12ff.), she needs various organizations. Yet she is not that. She is at no time anything but the Community of believers united through their Lord.

The Church, moreover, must never be understood on the basis of the proclaimed Word or the Sacraments. To be sure, the Church cannot come into being except through the pro-clamation of the Word (1 Cor. 3: 6ff.; 4: 15) and she does not stay alive save through baptism (Eph. 4: 5) and the Lord's Supper (1 Cor. 10: 16f.; 11: 20ff.). But to define the nature of the Church by saying, as has become customary since the Reformation, that the Church is there wherever the Word of God is rightly proclaimed and the Sacraments rightly admin-istered, is far from being the intention of the apostle Paul, the missionary of the Gentiles. He knows that there are also sermons which have neither inspired faith nor built up a Church (Acts 18: 6; 17: 18, 32). Far less is it his intention to say that the being of the Church is to be determined by the "office of proclamation". Of course, he does not leave anyone in doubt that the Church can only grow out of and exist by the service of the proclamation of the Gospel (1 Cor. 3: 10f.), that this service therefore constitutes an absolute life-necessity for the Church (Rom. 1: 14ff.; 2 Cor. 5: 18) as well as being a necessary expression of life (1 Cor. 9: 16f.), but never does he define the essence of the Church from that angle.

The Church is the true Israel (Rom. 11: 5ff.), that is, the chosen people of God (Rom. 9: 25), formed, growing and maintaining herself through the call to salvation, wherever the call is accepted in the obedience of faith (Rom. 1: 5; 15: 18). She is thus at the same time the Messianic Community in the twofold sense that she awaits the coming of Christ (1 Thess. 1: 10) and his glory (Phil. 3: 20) and that as the body of this head she belongs already to Christ and his new world (Col. 2: 19f.). She is the fellowship of Saints (Eph. 1: 15; 2: 19) namely the communion of those called out of this world by God (Rom. 9: 24; 1 Cor. 1: 2) and set apart (2 Cor. 6: 17) and renewed by the Holy Spirit (Eph. 4: 23), and of the people united with one another (1 Cor. 12: 13), whose membership in Christ and the new world era (Eph. 2: 6f.) shows itself by their living in a new way of life (Rom. 6: 4) and in their becoming and letting themselves be more and more sanctified towards the day of Jesus Christ (cp. *Sanctification*). Therefore the Church or Community stands over against the rest of the world, certain though it is that she now still exists in this world and shares in it through the "flesh" (1 Cor. 5: 10).

The first characteristic and fountainhead of the Church is the assembling together for divine worship, of which Paul, especially in the first letter to the Corinthians, gives us a clear picture (chapters 12 and 14). In this assembly everyone gives and takes; although everything ought to happen "orderly", there is no hard and fast rule. In the Community many services are necessary (1 Cor. 12: 7ff. and 28ff.)—it is not inappropriate to render the Pauline concept "service" by the idea of the "office" derived from the world of political law—which, partly entrusted to certain persons, partly according to the gifts bestowed by the Spirit, are freely taken over and exercised (Rom. 12: 6ff.). The apostle knows of no difference between clergy and laity. Every believer is a minister (Rom. 8: 5) and as a member has his responsibility and his task for the whole spiritual body (1 Cor. 14: 12). Individual men marked out for special tasks stand out from the rest of the Community; to name two, the apostles and prophets; and yet, in spite of the God-given authority which he asserts, the apostle also places himself on the same level with the individual believers (2 Cor. 1: 24). Even his word counts for nothing if it is his own, but only because and in so far as it is given to him by God through the Holy Spirit (Gal. 2: 7; 1 Cor. 7: 40). Paul bids the Communities examine his teaching and his instructions by applying this standard (2 Cor. 1: 12f.; 4: 2; 5: 11). Nowhere can one find a hint that a servant of the Church, simply by virtue of having been called to a special office, is in a position to exercise a spiritual authority which is also not continually examined for its spiritual genuineness (1 Cor. 16: 10; Rom. 16: 4).

The task of the Church is to live in the new life which she ✓ has in Jesus Christ and in the Holy Spirit, to keep alive this message about him and to spread it throughout the whole world (Mark 16: 15f.; 1 Thess. 1: 7ff.). The fellowship of believers is not merely one that is believed in but also one experienced in manifold ways (1 Thess. 5: 11ff.). It ought to be and is experienced in the mutual exchange of spiritual gifts (Rom. 1: 11f.), in mutual exhortation (Rom. 15: 14), in the common participation in divine worship (1 Cor. 14: 26) and the Lord's Supper (1 Cor. 10: 17; 11: 33), and in the active love of the brethren among themselves (Col. 1: 4). Yet it is also experienced from Community to Community (2 Cor. 8: 14) by visitation (2 Cor. 8: 24) and letter (Phil. 4: 1) through greetings and mutual aid (see the concluding sentences of the letters). Thus not only the fellowship in the individual congregation but also the fellowship of the body of Christ throughout the entire world becomes a reality (Rom. 15: 24-33), which indeed not only grows out of and exists by faith, but in its effect is similarly seen and perceived with joy and gratitude (2 Cor. 3: 2) as faith, hope and love (1 Thess. 1: 3).

All that Paul knows of an invisible Church is that the verdict on who is going to be acknowledged as a living member of the body in God's final judgment, belongs solely to God (1 Cor. 3: 13). Yet this reservation does not prevent Paul from expressly confirming that he sees the membership in Christ of the individual and the Communities as an object of his perception of faith (1 Thess. 1: 3; 2 Cor. 1: 24; 8: 7) drawing from it the conclusion that those who cannot be considered as having stood the test, according to this standard, are to be cut out of the Community (1 Cor. 5: 4f., 11). Paul still knows nothing of the fact that the Community normally consists of believers and hypocrites, though he certainly recognizes on the other hand that the final verdict concerning membership or non-membership belongs to God alone (1 Cor. 4: 4f.). Church discipline is the means whereby the Community preserves itself intact from elements that obviously do not belong to it (1 Cor. 5: 6f.). The aim of sanctification is to be blameless on the day of Jesus Christ; but perfection no one has as yet achieved, not even the apostle (cp. *Sanctification*).

LOVE

Even were there no thirteenth chapter of the first letter to the Corinthians, we should know that love, like grace and faith, stands at the centre of Paul's thought. First the love of God. Paul does not speak of it very often (Rom. 5: 5, 8; 8: 35) because he likes to designate it by a preciser concept: mercy (Rom. 12: 1; 2 Cor. 1: 3) or grace (see *Grace*). Love is an ambiguous word. For Paul it is unambiguously that which, at any rate in the philosophical thought of the Greeks and also in most religions which talk loftily of divine love, it is not: the immotivated love which gives, the love that loves "without any cause"! (Rom. 5: 8ff.). It is a love which loves, not because it finds something precious and worthy of being loved, but which just loves what is unworthy and worthless, and so makes it precious and worthy of love (Eph. 1: 5f.). The divine love condescends and gives itself (Rom. 8: 32) and that, not in order to find love in return, thus getting something back, but unconditionally (Rom. 9: 11-15).

Here lies the reason for Paul putting faith on man's side first instead of the love of God. For faith is the receiving of that love which God groundlessly bestows (Rom. 3: 22; Eph. 2: 8). And it is indeed the receiving of God's unconditional love. It does not first say: I love you if you love me too, but: I love you unconditionally, and at first demand only that you receive it, that you allow yourselves to be loved (2 Cor. 5: 20). To let oneself be loved unconditionally by God means to believe (1 Cor. 1: 21; Gal. 2: 20). Hence, out of this faith comes love (Phil. 2: 5; Gal. 5: 6).

Just as the Holy Spirit, God's Spirit, lives and works in believers, so God's own love also becomes effectual in them. It "has been poured into our hearts through the Holy Spirit" (Rom. 5: 5). This love is "the fulfilling of the Law" (Rom. 13:

10). It is this love whose nature and work Paul describes in the thirteenth chapter of the first letter to the Corinthians. Indeed, it is not human but divine love of which he speaks here; yet it is divine love as it is now already alive in believers (Col. 1: 4), and effective through them (2 Cor. 5: 14). We are not wrong in saying that Paul is speaking at this point of the "last things", the heavenly, eternal life. Yet we must add: this eternal life is present precisely as the new life through the Holy Spirit, even though only as a beginning. Where genuine faith is, there this love is also present (1 Thess. 3: 6; Gal. 5: 22; Eph. 3: 17), and in this love genuine faith must also show itself (Gal. 5: 6). That it actually does this, Paul gives testimony both of himself and of his Communities (Rom. 15: 14; Col. 1: 4, 8; 1 Thess. 1: 3; 3: 6).

Since it concerns the love of God it has also the quality of God's love; it is not covetous (1 Cor. 13: 5), it does not strive after what is precious or lofty, but it gives and strives for what is below (Rom. 12: 16). It does not inquire into the character of the recipient but it asks what he needs (Rom. 12: 13f., 20f.). It does not love him because he is such and such a person but because he is there. In all this it is quite the opposite of natural love: it "does not seek its own" (1 Cor. 13: 5). It does not perform the characteristic natural impulse of love and life. Therefore it is basically independent of the conduct of the other person (Rom. 12: 17, 21), it is not conditional but absolute. It wants nothing for itself but only for others (Phil. 2: 4). Therefore it is also not vulnerable. It never "reacts" but is always "spontaneous", emerging by its own strength— rather from the power of God (1 Cor. 13: 4ff.). Love is the real God-likeness of man for which he has been created (Col. 3: 10-14). In so far as love is in man he really resembles God and shows himself to be the child of God (Matt. 5: 45-48; Eph. 5: 1). This love is really human; that which is really human is thus the divine, as something that is simply received (Eph. 5: 2). Through it true fellowship is realized (Phil. 2: 2), in it man is only really free and creative (Eph. 3: 17ff.), it is the real life (Eph. 4: 15f.). It is therefore that which remains also in eternity (1 Cor. 13: 8) whereas faith and hope disappear as being merely temporary, transitory entities (1 Cor. 13: 13). Love is life from God (1 Cor. 8: 3), with God, for God, and life with and for other men (1 Thess. 4: 9). It is therefore the most precious of all the gifts of the Spirit (1 Cor. 12: 31) because it is itself the life of the Spirit (Rom. 15: 30; Col. 1: 8).

PREDESTINATION, ELECTION

As in the Bible in general, so also for Paul in particular the thought of free divine election is of decisive importance. Redemption, like Creation, is also quite solely the work of God and derived from his decree, from his free will (Eph. 1: 4). He makes what he will and how he will, he redeems whom he will and how he will. He is the Lord God, he is the Creator and has claims on his creatures; the creature however has none, not even the least claim on God. God is able to give and to refuse what he will. From the biblical way of thinking about God the concept of the free election of grace is a necessity (Rom. 9: 11-16).

Yet it is also necessary from the concept of salvation. Like the Bible in general, so Paul, too, knows of no other salvation of man except that God has mercy on him and establishes communion with him out of free love (Rom. 11: 5-7). God does not love because we are somehow worthy (1 Cor. 1: 27); but because God loves us, we have and are of value (1 Cor. 1: 30f.). His love, therefore, is totally "without foundation", "without a cause"; its sole reason is that God wills it (Rom. 9: 15f.). Thus his love is a free choice and this free choice, being the original cause of God's fellowship with us, is salvation (Eph. 2: 4-10). To have been chosen by God and to share in the salvation is therefore one and the same thing for Paul (2 Thess. 2: 13). Salvation is being elected, and being elected is salvation. For to be elected means to be loved, and to be loved means to be elected (Rom. 8: 29-33). And, what is more, it means having been elected from eternity (Eph. 1: 4-6, 9-12). What comes from God's will alone, comes out of eternity. If he loves us, then he loves us from eternity.

This electing, freely giving love of God has become manifest and effective in Jesus Christ (Eph. 1: 10). Indeed, having its origin in the eternal will of God, it is already united with the eternal Son (Eph. 1: 5). We have been chosen in the Son of God, from eternity (Col. 1: 13ff., 26ff.). And in Jesus Christ this love of God now apprehends us (Eph. 1: 11-13). Since we can see into God's heart and know his decree of love only through Jesus Christ (Col. 2: 2f.), although this decree has been made from eternity (Rom. 8: 29), so we know our election only in Jesus Christ (2 Thess. 2: 13f.). Faith is really nothing but to know and receive the eternal election of God in Jesus Christ (Eph. 1: 13). The chosen are therefore the same as the believers (Col. 3: 12), the same as those who belong to Christ through faith (Rom. 8: 33). For those whom he predestined he also called (Rom. 8: 30).

Has God therefore rejected others from eternity, namely, all those whom he does not predestine from eternity? This conclusion seems to be a logical necessity. The astonishing thing, however, which so many theologians of old and modern times have overlooked, is this: that neither Paul nor the Bible anywhere draw this conclusion. One does, indeed, read in the Bible as a whole, as also in Paul, much about those whom God rejects or has rejected (for example, Rom. 11: 15), but never about those whom he has rejected from eternity. One finds that God hardens men (Rom. 9: 18) but never that he has predestined them from eternity to hardness of heart. It is written in the letter to the Romans that God has the right to do with his creature what he will, that if he will he can also make vessels of wrath (Rom. 9: 20-22); but it does not say that he has predestined men from eternity to be vessels of wrath and created them as such. On the contrary, it is precisely those whom Paul describes in the ninth chapter as vessels of wrath (9: 22) of whom he says in the eleventh chapter that they are yet finally to be saved (11: 23ff.). In this matter Paul and the entire Bible are consistently illogical. The Scriptures refuse, as it were, to draw the conclusion which logic would like to draw from the concept of eternal election into the opposite direction. No part of the Bible approaches so closely the thought of a "double decree of predestination, one to salvation the other to damnation", as the ninth chapter of the letter to the Romans; on the other hand, however, none approximates so nearly to the doctrine of universal salvation as the end of the eleventh chapter. So illogical and contradictory is the biblical teaching!

If we ask why, then these are just the chapters to provide us with an answer: only the believer can know about election.

Faith, however, although being God's gift, is *commanded* us. We must believe (1 Cor. 16: 13; Col. 2: 7; Eph. 6: 16). The Word of Christ is being proclaimed to all nations, with the claim to obedience (Rom. 15: 18). What matters most is the decision of faith (Rom. 11: 20). Thus nothing theoretical is said about perdition as being something which "is there", but it comes only in an exhortation calling to repentance (Rom. 11: 20-22). If you do not believe, then you alone are to blame for it (Rom. 9: 32f.)—that is the teaching of the Bible. But if you believe, then you know it is entirely God's gift, his grace (Rom. 9: 16). Since it concerns the decision of faith to receive God's election through faith, the opposite of election is thus never predestination to perdition but unbelief, the possibility brought about by one's own fault and of which one is warned (Rom. 11: 23). Simply because the true life of man is entirely grounded in God alone and the false entity in sin alone, in the guilt of man, there is no logical symmetry here, and therefore the doctrine of election must necessarily be "illogical". And that it is, right through the whole of the Bible and all the Pauline letters. However frequently the eternal election is mentioned, there is never a word about an eternal determination to perdition, not even once (cp. for example Matt. 25: 34 with 25: 41). If we follow logic, if we draw from the doctrine of election the logical conclusion, then we are at variance with the basic thought of Holy Scripture that God is love. Although the opposite has in some way been continually asserted by theologians, it is impossible for any man to hold that God from eternity has predestined and created a number of people to perdition and that this God is love. Such a thing is said neither by Paul nor any other apostle or prophet; but: if God wants to save you, the sinner, then it is entirely his free mercy, and that he wants this he declares to you in Jesus Christ, and that it is which he bids you believe. If you do not wish to receive it, you are lost. One can only have the logical system of thinking at the price of losing the living and merciful God.

THE JUSTIFICATION OF THE SINNER

Whoever takes the will of God seriously must ask himself what God's judgment on him is, that kind of judgment God will pass on him when confronting him as the Judge. The Jews, to some extent, have taken this question seriously and have earnestly striven to keep to the Law as meticulously as possible (Rom. 10: 2). Yet they did not notice that they were not equal to it (Rom. 9: 31). Paul had first to come and make it clear to them that man cannot hold his own under God's judgment (Rom. 3: 23). But Paul as a Pharisee had not come to this realization. Only after Christ had shown him the new way was he able to see things as they are (Phil. 3: 4-7). Only then did it become clear to him that "we all have sinned and fallen short of the glory of God" (Rom. 3: 23), that we have each one of us therefore to fear the divine sentence of judgment, that we have to expect not praise but condemnation if there is to be a day of reckoning after all (Gal. 2: 16; 3: 11).

Yet it ought not to be like that. God in Jesus Christ has opened up another way (Rom. 3: 21). God declares the sinner righteous. Two things have to be asked in view of this. First, how can God call the evil man good? God does not do so. He does not say the evil man is good; God rather passes over this whole moral formulation of the question. Being good is of no importance to me now, he says; what matters to me is your being with me. Yet to you, the evil man, I say this: I am with you. I wish to have fellowship with you. I am your friend, I love you (Rom. 5: 6-10). God thus does not say that the sinner is no sinner, but that in spite of sin he desires to have fellowship with the sinner and does not let sin come between himself and men. He "covers" sin (Rom. 4: 5ff.). The second question is: why this difficult concept of justification? Why not simply "Forgiveness of sins"? This is how it is put in the Old Testament; Jesus has proclaimed it like this; the other apostles, too, say it in this way. What reason is there for using this abstruse expression when there exists already a much more understandable term for the same thing?

Certainly, justification of the sinner includes the forgiveness of sins. Yet it says still more. It says above all something positive, namely that God sets man in a new relation to himself. Forgiveness means: the separation through sin is being annulled. Justification says: man is being given a new dignity, a new basis of life. God affirms man in spite of his sin. Paul uses for it two other terms: "adoption of sons" (Rom. 8: 23; Gal. 4: 5) and "placing in the succession as heirs" (Rom. 8: 17; Gal. 4: 7).

But all this does not exhaust the content of the idea of justification. We must never forget when speaking of Paul's doctrine of justification that the concepts derived from the realm of law, to "justify", "to declare righteous", are like the other expressions all metaphors and cannot explain the matter exhaustively and therefore Paul puts them in apposition. Thus none of these metaphors, not even that of "justification", must be unduly pressed as if it contained in itself a self-explanatory doctrine or explanation of the new thing that happens to man through Jesus Christ. The same thing that Paul expresses by the "legal" term of justification and adoption he expresses just as frequently, or indeed still more often, by "mystical" metaphors such as "being in Christ" or "to grow together with Christ". Both, however dissimilar the "mystical" and the "legal" elements are in themselves, mean one and the same thing. Therefore Paul has not said everything when he uses the term *"declaring righteous"*. Concerning sinful man it is not only being stated from God's side that he is now righteous, but through union with Christ man actually becomes another. For he is now in Christ. And being thus united with God he receives the Holy Spirit (Rom. 8: 15; 5: 5). "If anyone is in Christ, he is a new creation" (2 Cor. 5: 17). He not only *believes* in a new life but in faith he *has* a new life (2 Cor. 13: 4; 4: 10f.). Faith is being joined to the quickening power of God (Col. 3: 3; Phil. 1: 21).

By believing in justification man is in the position of dependence on God, where God wants him to be. In faith man "is" as God intends him to be, he is righteous (Rom. 10: 10; 1 Cor. 6: 11; Rom. 6: 18). Thus what happens to us through Jesus Christ is not merely a being *declared* righteous, but on the basis of this, at the same time, a being *made* righteous (Eph. 4: 24).

In the Pauline doctrine of justification the biblical Gospel of grace attains its culminating point. The two main thoughts of the Gospel meet here, namely that all salvation lies in God's action and that salvation and condemnation consist in the relationship between God and man. The man who is right with God *has* salvation, and man is under condemnation when he is not right with God. Justification means: it is God alone who makes man stand in a right relation to him. God "puts" man right in justification. He alone can do it—for only he can exonerate him from guilt. And in this alone salvation is decreed, for "if God is for us who is against us?" (Rom. 8: 31). Justification, therefore, is by grace alone, or the "righteousness by faith" is the centre and climax of the biblical message.

SIN

The reason why the subject of sin stands so much in the foreground in the Bible and particularly in Paul, is that sin is the opposite of faith. Sin is the negative, the perverse relation to God. Man either lives by faith or in sin, just as he either sleeps or is awake, is dead or alive. There is no third alternative. Man either says Yes to God or No; he cannot say nothing; for even saying nothing, the flight from decision, is a decision—namely the negative one. Neutrality over against God is unbelief, pride and defiance. "He who is not with me is against me" (Matt. 12: 30). Sin is therefore not something that happens to man among other things now and then, something he does occasionally, but it is an entire way of life (Rom. 6: 16f.; Eph. 2: 1-3). Man is either in sin or he lives by faith (Rom. 6: 11, 20-22).

The question has frequently been raised as to whether for Paul sin is more a "condition" or an "act". This question is wrongly put. By "condition", of course, one means that which lasts, the thing which reaches beyond the individual moment and the individual decision of the will; by "act" is meant a conscious decision of the will which is at a certain moment changed into action. But for Paul sin is both. Sin is never anything but act, "transgression", "disobedience", a wrong direction of the will (Rom. 5: 12-14; 7: 7ff.), a false relationship, a wrong "attitude" towards God (Rom. 8: 7); yet at the same time it is never something merely momentary but always something determining the whole person in his unity, the "disposition" of the person (Rom. 7: 14ff.). Disposition and act here are not contradictory for Paul (Rom. 6: 16; Eph. 2: 3). The individual sins are, as it were, only the eruptions of this sin for ever bubbling in the deep (Rom. 7: 13; Col. 1: 21).

According to its nature sin is the opposite of the will of God;

thus it can be recognized by its opposition to the divine law (Rom. 3: 20; 7: 7). The occurrence of sin is the transgression of the Law, the root of sin is enmity against God (Rom. 5: 10; Col. 1: 21). Sin is like an enemy who is always planning something hostile even when he is not actually attacking (Rom. 8: 5ff.). Yet it is always, whether open or secret, contradiction against the divine will because of self-will. The divine will demands obedience, absolute dependence on God; human self-will demands just the opposite, freedom and independence (Rom. 6: 20). Therefore "the striving of the flesh"—that means the person cut off from God—is "enmity towards God" (Rom. 8: 7). This enmity can appear in the strangest disguises; for instance, morality and religion. It is able to hide behind zeal for the Law (Rom. 10: 3). It is precisely the legalism against which Paul fights his life's battle that he attacks as sin (Phil. 3: 1-7), as enmity against God (Rom. 11: 28) because the man of the Law simply wants to be righteous himself, of his own self. He wants to deserve the love of God instead of allowing it to be bestowed on him. This defiance is the real nature of sin.

Of course, Paul also knows ordinary common sin: greed, passion, undisciplined voluptuousness, unbridled desire, every degeneration of egoism and worldliness (cp. "the catalogue of vices" Rom. 1: 26ff.). But he traces them all back to their origin, the one root. Man does not want to give the honour to God (Rom. 1: 21). That sin must take on this palpable shape is brought about by the fact that man, if he turns away from God, must cling to the world (Rom. 1: 25; 2 Cor. 4: 4). It is thus also understandable why—afterwards, not originally—sin also is brought into a specially close relationship with physical sensuality, so that Paul can speak of the sinful members (Rom. 7: 5; Col. 3: 5) or the sinful body (Rom. 6: 6; Col. 2: 11). The really spiritual thing, the relation to God, the sinner has rejected, so that the sensual life remains for him as the field of his main activity. Yet Paul never accepts the view that the physical or sensual as such is sinful (1 Cor. 6: 19) in contrast to something "spiritual" which in itself might be good (Eph. 4: 18). Sin does not enter from the body into the spirit, but rather comes to the body from the spirit, in so far as we understand by spirit precisely the centre of personal decisions. A proscription or even only a depreciation of the physical as such is something alien to Paul, as it is to the whole of the Bible (1 Cor. 6: 15; Rom. 12: 1).

The source of sin is defection from God. Whose defection? Paul gives a twofold answer to this question: it is the defection of every individual man, and Adam's defection (Rom. 5: 12). For Paul mankind as a unity is summed up in Adam. Adam is important for Paul as the representative of the unity of the human race (Rom. 5: 17). Paul is not concerned with making clear the sin of individuals from the sin of the founder of the race through the doctrine of hereditary sin—if Paul had wanted that then he would have had to say more than what is written in Romans 5: 12. His sole aim is rather to demonstrate that everyone is involved in and has to bear the sin of the whole of humanity. The comparison between Adam and Christ (Rom. 5: 14) means that Christ confronts the whole of sinful humanity (Rom. 5: 18). We shall seek in vain in Paul for the doctrine of original sin as found in the later teaching of the Church. "Adam" for him is the term which is ready at his disposal for the one, sinful humanity, united in solidarity and reciprocal action (1 Cor. 15: 22), which became sinful not through God's creation but through its apostasy from it (Col. 3: 10; Eph. 4: 24).

Since for Paul the idea of sin is totally determined by the relationship to God, it goes without saying that guilt belongs to it even though he uses no special word for it (Rom. 3: 25; 1: 32; 4: 7 and 8). Guilt is the relationship to God destroyed by sin which man of himself is no longer able to restore. That which man has destroyed can no longer be made good, the curse can no longer be averted (Gal. 3: 10, 13) except by God Himself. Forgiveness is so important (Rom. 3: 25; Eph. 1: 7; Col. 1: 14) because sin is understood so entirely personally and so entirely from the relationship to God. The forgiveness, the "justification" of the sinner, is the restoration of the true relationship to God through God Himself (Rom. 4: 5ff.). Redemption must begin with it. The knowledge of sin, according to Paul, is derived from the Law (Rom. 3: 20). This does not mean, however, that it is possible without the intervention of Jesus Christ. God's verdict which judges and reveals is only to be understood in its profundity through the Christ-event, particularly through Christ's death on the Cross (Phil. 3: 10; Rom. 6: 2, 3, 8; Col. 3: 3).

BAPTISM

Paul did not refer often to baptism and expressly says that he himself was "not sent to baptize" and did only baptize a few people (1 Cor. 1: 14-17). But this does not mean that baptism is not of great importance. The few places that mention it are significant enough and the most important are to be found in the letter to the Romans. It goes without saying that Paul, like all the New Testament writings, presupposes everywhere adult baptism. This does not absolutely imply that children were not baptized—although we do not hear anything about it either from Paul or elsewhere in the New Testament, apart from one single reference which perhaps includes child baptism (Acts 16: 33, in addition 1 Cor. 1: 16). It does mean, however, that where Paul explains the significance of baptism he looks upon faith as its presupposition.

Paul assumes of all Christians that they have been baptized (Rom. 6: 3). Baptism, moreover, is also for him an event that is connected with the entry into the Christian Community (Eph. 4: 5; 1 Cor. 12: 13). And, what is more, it is not only a symbolical ceremony portraying something, no matter what else might happen or be present; it is rather a real event between Christ and man (Rom. 6: 3) and between the individual members of the Community. "For by one Spirit we were all baptized into one body" (1 Cor. 12: 13). Not baptism but Jesus Christ or the Holy Spirit is the one who brings about this union (Eph. 5: 26; 1 Cor. 12: 13). But he makes use here of the means of baptism. The Holy Spirit, however, according to the teaching of the apostle, becomes effective only through Word and faith. Through faith we receive the Holy Spirit, never otherwise (Gal. 3: 2, 5). Thus the uniting of the individual with the Community by means of baptism can only happen where Word and faith are present (Eph. 5: 26; Col. 2: 12). Baptism and faith belong necessarily together.

Although Paul sees in certain incidents of Old Testament history (1 Cor. 10: 1ff.; Col. 2: 11) an allusion to baptism, this "Sacrament" for him is unmistakably based upon the historical fact of the death and the resurrection of Jesus. Baptism is a being placed into the death of Christ (Rom. 6: 3; Col. 2: 12). As Jesus Himself called his death a baptism (Mark 10: 38; Luke 12: 50), so Paul now reversely calls the baptism of Christians a dying (Rom. 6: 8). But as the death of Jesus is not just any death, but the death on the Cross, the death of atonement, the death which was suffered for the sin of mankind, so baptism, too, is the sharing in, in fact the union with this death for sin (Rom. 6: 10f.). In baptism the old man is "buried" (Col. 2: 12), "crucified" (Rom. 6: 6) or "put off" (Eph. 4: 22) and sin thereby washed away (1 Cor. 6: 11).

But just as in the history of Christ, death and resurrection form an inseparable unity—"if Christ be not raised then your faith is in vain" (1 Cor. 15: 14)—so baptism, too, is not merely the dying with Christ but also the rising with him (Col. 2: 12; Rom. 6: 4). The believer is "anointed" with the Holy Spirit (2 Cor. 1: 21) and "sealed" (Eph. 1: 13), he is also linked in baptism through the Holy Spirit to the living Christ in a union of life (Rom. 6: 11). "But he who is united to the Lord becomes one spirit with him" (1 Cor. 6: 17). In being united with Christ, however, through the Holy Spirit, he also becomes incorporated into the Community, the mysterious body of Christ (Col. 3: 15).

How far this is the effect of baptism itself or of faith in the word of the Cross, how far therefore the fact of man becoming new is linked to baptism as an external act, Paul does not explain. He simply gives to baptism, which he found to be a custom practised in the Community as a matter of course, this interpretation, spending no more time over whether baptism is "necessary for salvation" or not. But what is fully and clearly excluded by him is the magical understanding of baptism that came into vogue in the later Church, where, by virtue of an external act carried out by a priest, the Holy Spirit is infused into the baptized infant and whereby without faith playing any part, sin would be washed away and the new life conferred. However realistically Paul speaks of the mysterious operation of the Spirit in baptism, he still always clearly expresses the need for faith and repentance in and for this event. What Paul would have said from that position regarding the later custom of child baptism is hard to say. The children of believers count for him indeed as sanctified through the faith of the parents (1 Cor. 7: 14), but there is no connection here with baptism, any more than there is to be found in Paul (in spite of Col. 2: 11) a special reference to the Old Testament circumcision of the new-born boy. Baptism and faith belong together in the same way as the gift of the Holy Spirit is bound to faith.

THE WRATH OF GOD AND RECONCILIATION

The conception of the wrath of God appears to many as being a contradiction of the thought that God is love (1 Jn. 4: 16). They would thus very much like to erase the phrase "wrath of God" from the Bible. This, however, could not happen without destroying the entire biblical message. Therefore the concept of God's wrath, especially in the letter to the Romans, finds its necessary place in Paul (Rom. 1: 18; 2: 5; 4: 15 and elsewhere). God is the Holy One, he "is not mocked, for whatever a man sows that he will also reap" (Gal. 6: 7). If obedience to the will of God is salvation, then disobedience toward him is damnation. If being united with him is life, then separation from him is death (Rom. 5: 12ff.; 6: 16ff.; 7: 5, etc.). We stand in need of deliverance and a deliverer, since in separation from God we live in sin, are condemned and face damnation (Rom. 5: 18; Eph. 2: 3ff.; Col. 1: 13). By necessity the bridge belongs to the chasm which it spans: to Christ the Saviour necessarily belongs evil from which he is to save us. If there were no evil we would need no Saviour.

Evil is grounded in sin (Rom. 8: 6; 6: 23). The effect of evil is that we stand in a perverted relationship to God (Rom. 8: 7f.). Thus God, seen from our side, stands also now in the wrong relationship to us. His true relationship to his human children, the relationship that exists through him, is love (Rom. 5: 6ff.). Sin, however, turns this relationship into wrath (Rom. 1: 18). God's wrath is, as it were, the "head wind" which everyone who runs in opposition to God is made to feel. God, of course, does not want to be angry, to punish and destroy, but the opposite (2 Pet. 3: 9; 1 Tim. 2: 4; Luke 19: 10). But sin leads man into the position where God's holiness cannot become effective in him in any other way than by being harmful, whereas it would like to operate savingly (Rom. 8: 13). Whoever runs against

God must dash himself to pieces on God (Gal. 6: 7f.). If it were not so, then God would not be God, and his will would not be a holy will.

God's wrath, moreover, is never God's attitude to us; that shows itself, of course, in his giving to us, the sinners, the Saviour and that in him he also loves us, the sinners (Rom. 5: 6-8). Rather the wrath of God is the effect of his holiness under which we stand so long as we are against him. Salvation and damnation are not as yet decided and final; both are only in the state of becoming, in the critical balance (Rom. 2: 4). Thus the full effect of the damnation is still outstanding, just as also the full effect of the saving redemption (Rom. 2: 5). The last judgment, the final decision which ultimately divides, is still to come (Eph. 5: 6; 1 Thess. 1: 10). Therefore God's wrath is mentioned especially in view of this disastrous future event, yet not exclusively. Indeed even now the wrath of God is revealed and operative (Rom. 1: 18; 1 Thess. 2: 16), even if as yet not in its full force. But, just because it is mitigated through God's forbearance, man ought to use the time of decision as a time for repentance and be converted before the wrath (Rom. 2: 4) as had already been preached by John the Baptist and before him by the Prophets of Israel.

Therefore, since matters regarding God's wrath stand thus, reconciliation is not indeed to be understood as a reconciliation *of God*. Paul knows nothing of Christ's sacrifice as a means for reconciling God. Where he mentions reconciliation, he speaks of the reconciliation *of men* through Jesus Christ (Rom. 5: 10; 2 Cor. 5: 18). God Himself has not first to be reconciled; it is indeed he himself who sends the deliverer, he himself is the deliverer (Col. 1: 13). His love is the love of Christ, his love is meant for the sinner, for him who has deserved the wrath and stands under wrath (Rom. 5: 6-10). The atoning sacrifice of Christ does not overcome God's wrath in the same way as an angry tyrant is placated and favourably influenced by gifts. God does not receive a gift, he bestows Christ on us and in him he gives himself (Rom. 8: 32). The reconciliation does not overcome God's enmity but ours (Eph. 2: 14). It is the confirmation of what we rightly said concerning God's wrath, namely, that it is not God's attitude towards us but the effect which God's holiness has upon those who are against him. At the moment when they are no longer against him, when they are reconciled, this effect of wrath ceases too: they stand no longer under wrath but under grace (Rom. 5: 9f.).

But this victory over the enmity of men, this reconciliation, cannot happen from man's side. It requires the divine intervention, the divine act of atonement (Rom. 3: 25). Something "lies" between God and man and it is this which must be removed. And its removal costs nothing less than Jesus Christ (Col. 1: 22). The disturbance in the relationship between God and man is so deep that it can be overcome only by this opposite event, this act of making good which God Himself carries out instead of man (Col. 2: 14). The loving God reconciles hostile man to himself, removing thereby the wrath of God, the effect which God's holiness must exercise against perverse man (Eph. 2: 13f.). There is now one way out of the condemnation into which sin has plunged man and which he goes to face on the day of judgment: Jesus Christ (Rom. 3: 21). Whoever lets himself be apprehended by him in faith (Rom. 3: 22) no longer stands under the wrath of God; he is reconciled, delivered from his opposition against God and thereby also from the evil of this opposition (Col. 1: 20ff.). Whoever does not believe, remains under wrath (Rom. 9: 22; 11: 7).

Yet this, too, is not said to us "theoretically" but as the faith-demanding word of God. God's will is not wrath but grace for all (Rom. 11: 32). He, however, who does not surrender himself in faith to God's reconciling grace in Jesus remains God's enemy and continues to live under the state of wrath (Rom. 11: 23). Moreover, the reconciliation that has taken place for all in Christ and is offered to all in the Gospel, is not thrust upon us; we have to decide for it ourselves (2 Cor. 3: 16). Reconciliation is not a fate that happens to one but God's word calling us to faith. For the Gospel of Jesus Christ is "a power of God for the salvation of all who believe in it."